Sobriety

Sobriety
A Graphic Novel

Daniel D. Maurer
Illustrated by Spencer Amundson

HAZELDEN®

Hazelden
Center City, Minnesota 55012
hazelden.org

Library of Congress Cataloging-in-Publication Data

Maurer, Daniel D., 1971-
  Sobriety : a graphic novel / Daniel D Maurer ; illustrated by Spencer Amundson.
     pages cm
  Includes bibliographical references.
  ISBN 978-1-61649-557-2 (paperback) —ISBN 978-1-61649-568-8 (e-book)
1. Alcoholics—Rehabilitation—United States—Comic books, strips, etc. 2. Addicts—Rehabilitation—United States—Comic books, strips, etc. 3. Twelve-step programs—Comic books, strips, etc. 4. Graphic novels. I. Amundson, Spencer. II. Title.
  HV5275.M28 2014
  362.2920973—dc23

                                                                    2014031137

Editor's note

This publication is not intended as a substitute for the advice of health care professionals.

Alcoholics Anonymous, AA, and the Big Book are registered trademarks of Alcoholics Anonymous World Services, Inc.

Hazelden offers a variety of information on addiction and related areas. The views and interpretations expressed herein are those of the author and are neither endorsed nor approved by AA or any Twelve Step organization.

The Twelve Steps are reprinted from *Alcoholics Anonymous,* 4th ed. (New York: Alcoholics Anonymous World Services, 2001), 59–60.

The quote on page 66 is from *Narcotics Anonymous,* 6th ed. (Van Nuys, CA: Narcotics Anonymous World Services, 2008), 17.

The quote on page 86 is from *Alcoholics Anonymous,* 4th ed. (New York: Alcoholics Anonymous World Services, 2001), 56; emphasis added.

The quote on page 101 is from Bill W.'s letter to Dr. Carl Gustav Jung, January 23, 1961; emphasis added.

The quote on page 104 is from Carl Jung's letter to Bill W., January 30, 1961.

The Promises on pages 127–128 are reprinted from *Alcoholics Anonymous,* 4th ed. (New York: Alcoholics Anonymous World Services, 2001), 83–84.

The quote on page 134 is reprinted from *Alcoholics Anonymous,* 4th ed. (New York: Alcoholics Anonymous World Services, 2001), 58.

The quote on page 143 is reprinted from *Twelve Steps and Twelve Traditions,* 48th printing (New York: Alcoholics Anonymous World Services, 2009), 106.

18 17 16 15 14 1 2 3 4 5 6

Acknowledgments

I would like to extend my most sincere appreciation and acknowledgments to the following people: to Spencer Amundson, my artist, without whose dedication and creativity this work would not exist; to Maddi Gonzalez for contributing her fine artwork in the metalayer depicting the World War II scenes; to Carl Thompson, my letterer, with whom I was fortunate to connect; to Wendy Sherer, my American contact and deejay-in-residence in London, for her studious and fine research into the dialects and lingo used by locals in England; to Brenda Anfinson, my proficient translator for Mexican-American Spanish; to Sid Farrar, my editor at Hazelden Publishing, for his tireless encouragement and vision to see the potential of this book to change lives; to April Ebb, for coordinating the copyediting and proofreading; to my AA and NA sponsors, both present and past, for their guidance and support; and lastly, to my wife Carol, my parents, my in-laws, and my boys, Joshua and Nathan, for believing in me—when I failed to see the light, you showed me the spark still glowing inside and helped me rediscover the fire in my belly to effect change in the world.

— Daniel D. Maurer

HI. MY NAME IS *DAN*.
I'M AN *ALCOHOLIC AND AN ADDICT*.
I'M ALSO IN RECOVERY.
I'M *SOBER, JUST FOR TODAY*.

YOU MIGHT BE WONDERING WHAT I'M DOING ON A BLANK PAGE.

AFTER ALL, AREN'T OUR LIVES FILLED WITH A SENSE OF *PLACE AND TIME*?

THAT'S THE GREAT THING ABOUT THIS...

...AND IT'S *WORTHWHILE*.

SO WE'RE GOING TO SHOW YOU A WORLD THAT IS REALLY DIFFERENT FROM WHAT YOU'VE *BECOME USED TO*...

...AND THE *MAGIC* OF COMICS WILL ALLOW YOU TO SEE THIS IN A DIFFERENT WAY THAN YOU MIGHT HAVE SEEN IT IN THE PAST!

KCK!

WE'RE INVITING YOU TO TAKE THIS LITTLE *EXCURSION*, THIS *JOURNEY*, THIS *GLOBE-TROTTING ODYSSEY* WITH US. OH! I KEEP SAYING "US" AND "WE." I GUESS I NEED TO INTRODUCE...

...THE ARTIST, *SPENCER*!

EEEEEE

SPENCER'S THE ONE WHO GIVES THIS WORLD *REALITY*...

...WHILE *I'M* THE ONE WHO GIVES IT *BODY* AND *WORDS*.

HE'LL JOIN US LATER TO PUT THIS STORY INTO PERSPECTIVE.

NOW, WE NEED TO GET TO THE *REAL* STORY... THE STORY THAT WILL HOPEFULLY PUT SOME LITERARY SUSTENANCE TO WHAT THE *TWELVE STEPS* ARE AND WHY THEY ARE CENTRAL TO *SOBRIETY*.

BECAUSE, AS WE ADDICTS KNOW, *SOBRIETY* ISN'T JUST ABOUT PUTTIN' A *CORK IN THE BOTTLE* OR *STAYIN' AWAY FROM DRUGS*.

SOBRIETY IS MORE THAN THE DEFINITION WE FIND IN THE *DICTIONARY*. IT'S A *NEW LIFESTYLE* THAT WE EMBRACE.

IT GIVES US *A REAL EXISTENCE*. IT'S WHOLLY DIFFERENT FROM WHAT WE EXPERIENCE IN OUR ADDICTION.

THE *TWELVE STEPS*! THEY REALLY AREN'T ALL THAT *WEIRD*...

THEY JUST TAKE A LITTLE *GETTING USED TO*.

SO I INVITE YOU TO *JOIN* US!

COME ON... THERE ARE SOME PEOPLE I'D LIKE YOU TO MEET.

MEET *LARRY*.

HE'S IN RECOVERY TOO. LARRY LOST HIS WIFE TO CANCER TWO YEARS AGO...

...BUT HE'S STILL LIVING A LIFE OF *SOBRIETY* AND *FREEDOM*.

LARRY IS MUCH MORE THAN HIS LIFE'S WORK.

HE IS MORE THAN THE SUM OF HIS EXPERIENCES.

HE HAS MANY COLORS TO HIS PAST. THEY ARE LIKE PAINT TO A WHITE CANVAS...ALL THE THINGS THAT GIVE HIM A *PLACE*, A *TIME*...THAT WHICH GIVES HIM *MEANING AND VALUE* IN THIS WORLD.

LARRY'S BEEN AT AA MEETINGS FOR OVER THIRTY YEARS.

IT'S BEEN GOOD, BUT HE'S HAD HIS SHARE OF PROBLEMS TOO.

NOW...

CLICK!

HE'S GOING TO JOIN OTHERS...

LIKE HE ALWAYS DOES...

...TO KEEP HIMSELF *SOBER*.

THAT'S WHAT HE DOES IN HIS *NEW* LIFE... ...HIS *SOBER* LIFE.

IT'S SOMETHING HE'S COME TO LOVE.

AND WE HOPE YOU'LL COME TO LOVE YOUR NEW LIFE TOO!

HERE'S **DEBBY**.

SHE'S THE MOTHER OF TWO LITTLE BOYS. SHE HATES HER JOB — IT DRIVES HER NUTS. SHE'S FROM FLORIDA. THIS IS HER THIRD TREATMENT FOR BENZOS AND ALCOHOL.

SHE'S GOING TO A SPEAKER'S MEETING — THAT'S WHERE SOMEBODY WHO'S SOBER SHARES THEIR STORY WITH YOU.

RM2017

WHY IS DEBBY SO **AT EASE**?

AFTER ALL, SHE WAS A SHAKING MESS JUST FOUR WEEKS AGO...

AND HERE'S DEBBY **TWO MONTHS** AGO...

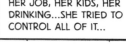

YOU MIGHT BE ABLE TO RELATE.

HER JOB, HER KIDS, HER DRINKING...SHE TRIED TO CONTROL ALL OF IT...

AND **MANAGE** IT...

...AND MAKE IT **RIGHT**.

BUT SHE FOUND OUT THAT SHE COULDN'T DO IT HERSELF. AT SOME POINT, SHE WAS **WILLING TO GIVE UP** AND **WORK** THE TWELVE STEPS. IT WASN'T EASY, THOUGH.

LOOK AT *MATT*.
HE'S THE LOST PUP IN THE MIDDLE IN THE T-SHIRT.
MATT HAS HAD QUITE A RUN IN LIFE. HIS POISON
OF CHOICE IS *CRYSTAL METH*.

HE HAD A *BIG PARTY* BEFORE HE ENDED UP HERE...

...HOSTED BY THE *STATE OF CALIFORNIA*!

YOU'D NEVER KNOW THAT MATT'S AN ADDICT, JUST SEEING HIM ON THE STREET. DRUGS ARE LIKE THAT — FIRST YOU FEEL CONFIDENT AND GLOWING, BRAND SPANKING NEW. THEN, THAT OL' SNAKE SLITHERS AND THE BUGS CRAWL AND...

...THE HAMMER *DROPS*!

I *KNOW* THEY'RE OUT THERE!

BUT THEN HE'S OUT AGAIN...BUYING AND USING, SCAMMING AND STEALING, SCORING AND BANGING...UNTIL...

SLAM CLANK

NO ONE *WANTS* TO BE HERE. NONE OF US *PLANNED* THIS...

MEET *HANNAH*. SHE'S EIGHTEEN AND THE YOUNGEST ONE OF THE BUNCH.

SHE ISN'T TOO HAPPY TO BE HERE. OF COURSE, MANY AREN'T.

SHE *SURPRISED* HER PARENTS. NO, *SHOCKED* IS MORE LIKE IT.

AFTER ALL, YOU DON'T EXPECT AN *HONORS STUDENT*...

...TO END UP HERE.

BUT, ISN'T THAT WHAT *LIFE* AT *EIGHTEEN* IS ABOUT? PARTIES? *FUN?*

FUN? LIKE *LIFTING PAIN MEDS* FROM YOUR PARENTS' FRIENDS?

BUT, AS WE ALL KNOW...

...EVERY PARTY ALWAYS COMES *TO AN END*.

THING IS, SHE'S AN ADULT. HER PARENTS CAN'T TELL HER WHAT TO DO!

YEAH. RIGHT...

AH, HERE'S ALEX. HE'S FROM THE UK, BUT HE'S LIVING IN A SOBER HOUSE NOW. THAT'S A HOUSE WHERE A PERSON LIVES WITH OTHER ADDICTS — PEOPLE IN RECOVERY.

HE'S STILL NOT *FULLY* HIMSELF, HAVING ONLY SIX MONTHS OF DRUG-FREE TIME.

ALEX NEVER THOUGHT HE'D BE COMING *THIS FAR* FROM HOME. HE COULD HAVE STAYED IN LONDON, BUT HE HAS RELATIVES IN THE STATES.

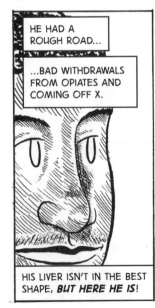

HE HAD A ROUGH ROAD...

...BAD WITHDRAWALS FROM OPIATES AND COMING OFF X.

HIS LIVER ISN'T IN THE BEST SHAPE, *BUT HERE HE IS*!

THAT'S WHAT IT'S LIKE FOR MOST ALCOHOLICS AND ADDICTS — WE'RE IN TOUGH SHAPE, BUT WE DO GET *BETTER. YOU WILL TOO.*

LET'S LISTEN IN ON LARRY'S STORY. I SEE THAT EVERYBODY'S SEATED.

I'VE COME HERE TODAY AS A SERVICE OPPORTUNITY...NO, IT'S NOT JUST AN OPPORTUNITY...IT'S— IT'S A...

...*A NECESSITY!* IT'S THAT I *HAVE TO* SHARE. *YOU* ARE THE REASON THAT I STAY SOBER! BECAUSE OF THE NATURE OF THIS PROGRAM, I WANT TO *GIVE AWAY* WHAT I'VE RECEIVED.

YOU SEE, I WANT TO SHARE WITH YOU MY EXPERIENCE, STRENGTH, AND HOPE...THAT ADDICTION DOESN'T HAVE TO HAVE THE LAST SAY IN OUR LIVES. YOU SEE, ADDICTION ISN'T JUST IN OUR *HEADS* — IT'S IN OUR *BODIES* AND OUR *SPIRITS* TOO. THAT'S A FACT THAT WAS HARD FOR ME TO ACCEPT. AS AN ALCOHOLIC I WILL ALWAYS "*HAVE IT*" — BUT IT DOESN'T NEED TO *HAVE ME!*

I'M HERE TODAY BECAUSE I WANT TO *STAY WELL*. IT'S A PLEASURE FOR ME TO SHARE MY STORY WITH YOU, BECAUSE I KNOW YOU'LL RECOGNIZE *YOUR OWN STORY* WHEN I SHARE MINE. MY LIFE AND MY EXPERIENCE ARE DIFFERENT FROM YOURS, BUT OUR *DISEASE* IS THE SAME: PUT A *DROP* OF BOOZE OR MOOD-ALTERING CHEMICALS IN US AND *WE CHANGE*. WE BECOME THAT WHICH WE *NEVER THOUGHT WE WOULD:*

MANIPULATIVE, LYING, STEALING, SELF-CENTERED PEOPLE...

...ONLY HEADED FOR *JAILS, INSTITUTIONS, OR DEATH!*

I CAME TO A PLACE IN LIFE WHERE MAYBE YOU FOUND YOURSELVES TOO — INCREDIBLE DESPERATION TO *DO ANYTHING* TO ESCAPE THE HELL OF ADDICTION. BECAUSE I KNEW "*IT*" WASN'T THE *CORE* OF *WHO I AM!*

15

THERE WAS A WELL-KNOWN PSYCHIATRIST WHO, AFTER HE HAD EXHAUSTED ALL POSSIBLE AVENUES WITH ONE OF HIS LONG-TERM PATIENTS, SUGGESTED THAT THE ONLY CURE HE COULD FIND FOR THE PATIENT'S CHRONIC CONDITION WOULD BE A "VITAL SPIRITUAL EXPERIENCE." THIS PATIENT RETURNED TO HIS COUNTRY OF ORIGIN (HE HAD TRAVELED A GREAT DISTANCE TO SEE THE DOCTOR) AND SET OUT TO HAVE A PERSONAL CONVERSION EXPERIENCE TO CURE HIS CONDITION.

BECAUSE THE DOCTOR SUGGESTED TO THE MAN THAT HIS CURRENT AFFILIATION WITH HIS CHURCH DID NOT CONSTITUTE A "VITAL" SPIRITUAL EXPERIENCE, THE MAN SOUGHT THROUGH SEVERAL AVENUES TO SOLVE HIS PROBLEM. HE EVENTUALLY FOUND A GROUP OF PEOPLE WHO WERE COMMITTED TO A NEW WAY OF LIFE THOROUGHLY DIFFERENT FROM THE OLD. THEY CALLED THEMSELVES THE OXFORD GROUP. THIS NEW WAY OF LIFE, HE WAS TOLD, WOULD DIRECTLY ADDRESS THE SOURCE OF HIS PROBLEM AND HIS AILMENT.

ALTHOUGH THE EARLY HISTORY IS FUZZY AS TO WHAT TRANSPIRED FOR THIS MAN IN THE EARLY YEARS, HE EVENTUALLY FOUND THAT HIS QUALITY OF LIFE WAS GREATLY IMPROVED. HE SOON INVITED ANOTHER MAN TO THE OXFORD GROUP TO FIND A SOLUTION FOR HIS COMMON AILMENT. THIS MAN, WHO WENT BY EBBY, FOUND, INITIALLY AT LEAST, THAT THE GROUP HAD SOLVED HIS PROBLEMS. EBBY WAS GOOD FRIENDS WITH **BILL W.,** THE MAN WHO WOULD GO ON TO ESTABLISH THE **TWELVE STEPS** AND COFOUND **ALCOHOLICS ANONYMOUS.**

THIS IS HOW IT BEGAN... **ONE PERSON TO ANOTHER.** THIS IS HOW IT WORKS TODAY.

THE AILMENT, OF COURSE, WAS **ALCOHOLISM.**

BUT WE KNOW THAT IT'S THIS WAY FOR **ADDICTS** TOO. OUR MINDS AND BODIES — AND **OUR SPIRITS** — THEY ARE BROKEN. AND WE AREN'T LIKE OTHER *NORMAL* PEOPLE.

I NEEDED TO FIND SOMETHING TO MAKE ME FEEL NORMAL AGAIN. FOR ME, THAT WAS A CONNECTION TO THE **INFINITE**...MY **HIGHER POWER.**

FOR THOSE OF US WHO SUFFER FROM THE **SCOURGE** OF **ADDICTION,** I DISCOVERED THAT A RICH, **SPIRITUAL LIFE** WAS WHAT I NEEDED.

SPIRITUALITY USED TO **SCARE** ME... LIKE IT WAS ONLY SOMETHING FOR GURUS AND PRIESTS.

BUT I CAME TO UNDERSTAND THAT SPIRITUALITY **ISN'T WHAT I THOUGHT IT WAS!**

I DIDN'T THINK **SPIRITUALITY** "FIT" WHO I WAS, THAT IT WAS ABOUT **WEIRD** THINGS. BUT WHAT IT'S REALLY ABOUT IS PRETTY **EASY:** IT'S ABOUT **LIVING LIFE A NEW WAY!**

IT'S ABOUT LIVING BY LIFE'S TERMS, AND NOT BY OURS.

I FOUND THAT SEEING IT THIS WAY MADE A **BIG DIFFERENCE** TO **ME!**

St. Paul, Minnesota — 1946

IT'S BEEN A LONG JOURNEY...

Midway Neighborhood — St. Paul

I WAS BORN IN ST. PAUL, JUST AFTER WWII. MY MOM WAS A NURSE. MY DAD HAD BEEN IN THE WAR, FIGHTING IN THE PACIFIC. COMING HOME WASN'T EASY FOR HIM.

I THINK DAD WAS THE TYPE OF PERSON WHO LIKED **CHALLENGE** AND **ADVENTURE** IN LIFE. THE WAR HAD GIVEN HIM THAT.

HOME LIFE DIDN'T.

17

SO, EVEN THOUGH THE WAR WAS HARD FOR HIM — WONDERING IF HIS SHIP WOULD EVER END UP IN THE BOWELS OF SOME PACIFIC TRENCH —

IT WAS ALSO SOMETHING *EXCITING* AND *DIFFERENT*.

KR-KOOM!

KR-KOOM!

COMING HOME WAS MUCH HARDER. LIFE IN A TIDY STUCCO BUNGALOW ON THOMAS AVENUE IN THE MIDWAY NEIGHBORHOOD — WITH THREE BOYS, A WIFE, AND A POODLE — WITH ALL ITS WORK AND ROUTINE, BECAME TERRIBLY *MUNDANE* AND *BORING* FOR HIM.

SO DAD *SUPPLEMENTED* HIS TEDIOUS FAMILY LIFE WITH MORE *ADVEN-TURE* — NOT IN A HEALTHY WAY WITH A HOBBY OR SOMETHING GOOD, BUT BY SWAMPING HIS BRAIN WITH WHISKEY, GIN, AND BOURBON.

I THINK HE LOOKED FORWARD TO THIS TIME AT ONE OF ST. PAUL'S MANY *FINE ESTABLISHMENTS*, PERCHED ON THE CORNER OF NEARLY EVERY BLOCK.

WHEN HE GOT HOME, *HIS MAJESTY* SLUMPED ONTO HIS *ROYAL THRONE* — A ROUGH PLAID RECLINER IN THE LIVING ROOM.

DAD WORKED AT THE FORD PLANT IN THE CITY. I DON'T THINK HE LIKED HIS JOB MUCH. BUT, HEY, AT LEAST IT GAVE HIM **MONEY**...

...**MONEY** TO **DRINK** HIS TROUBLES *AWAY*. DAY-TO-DAY LIVING FOR OUR FAMILY BECAME AN EXERCISE IN SURVIVAL.

SO...I LEARNED TO MIND MY OWN BUSINESS. THAT WAS "*JUST DAD.*"

ANYONE LIVING WITH AN ALCOHOLIC KNOWS THAT EVERY DRUNK EXPRESSES THEIR FRUSTRATION IN DIFFERENT WAYS.

AHEM.

UH, DAD, COULD I PLEASE HAVE FIVE BUCKS FOR THE WINTER CARNIVAL?

IF YOU WANT MONEY, WHY DON'T YOU GET A **GODDAMN JOB**?! GO OUT AND, AND... SHOVEL SNOW OR SOMETHIN'!

I SHOULD **NEVER** HAVE BOTHERED DAD...

YOU. C'MERE!

BAM!

AFTER A USUAL ASSAULT OF **PUT-DOWNS** OR A TRIP TO THE **PROVERBIAL WOODSHED**, I'D LICK MY WOUNDS AND PROMISE MYSELF I'D THINK TWICE BEFORE I ASKED DAD ANYTHING.

I WORK ALL DAY FOR *THIS SLOP*?! YOU OVERCOOK EVERYTHING! WHY CAN'T YOU...

DISGUSTING *DRUNK*!

MOM TOOK THE BRUNT OF DAD'S ABUSE TOO. I NEVER SAW HIM HIT HER. NOT ONCE. BUT ALL THE TIME HE *ASSAULTED* HER WITH *PUT-DOWNS*, *DEGRADING REMARKS*, OR *YELLING*.

IT WAS EVIDENT THAT MY PARENTS LIVED A MARRIAGE OF CONVENIENCE.

ALCOHOL WAS MY DAD'S ONE TRUE LOVE.

AT BOTH SCHOOL AND AT HOME, I LOST MYSELF IN BOOKS.

I WASN'T THE BEST STUDENT, SINCE SOME SUBJECTS WERE DIFFICULT FOR ME.

THAT'S EXACTLY IT, LARRY!

THERE WAS ONE TEACHER, THOUGH, WHO SAW MY TALENT FOR READING AND NURTURED IT.

FICTION WAS A WAY FOR ME TO ESCAPE INTO *ANOTHER WORLD*. I WOULD LOSE MYSELF AND ALL MY SHAME, INSECURITY, AND FEAR IN THOSE BOOKS. I WOULD LET TIME SLIP AWAY IN THE PAGES OF OTHER WORLDS. *READING* WAS A *LIFE-LONG GIFT* I GREW TO CHERISH. THAT IS, UNTIL I FOUND *SOME-THING ELSE*...

GODDAMN, FUCKING PIECE OF SHIT...

THERE WERE TIMES WHEN I WANTED TO ESCAPE THE CHAOS IN MY HOUSE INSTEAD OF READING. I WOULD *SNEAK OUT* WHEN MY DAD WOULD YELL. I'D MAKE MY WAY IN THE DIM MOONLIGHT TO AN EMPTY PARK.

I USED TO LOVE THAT PARK. IT HAD A FAKE FIBERGLASS BALLISTIC MISSILE AS A JUNGLE GYM FOR KIDS. (WE WERE LIVING IN THE COLD WAR, AFTER ALL.) I DIDN'T LIKE GOING DURING THE DAY. THERE WERE TOO MANY KIDS THEN. I LOVED THE PLACE BECAUSE, TO ME, IT WAS A *REFUGE* AWAY FROM THE *CHAOS* AT HOME.

WHEN I THINK BACK ON IT...

ONE EVENING WHEN I WANTED A BREAK FROM DAD'S TIRADE AND THE DRAMA IN OUR HOUSE, I STRUGGLED UP THE STAIRS AND MADE MY WAY ACROSS THE GANGPLANK ATTACHED TO THE MISSILE.

I LIKED THE MISSILE BECAUSE IT WAS WAY UP IN THE AIR AND I HAD A CLEAR VIEW OF THE NIGHT SKY.

THAT NIGHT, I WATCHED DIM, POWDERY ANGELS CAST THEIR VEIL ACROSS THE SPARKLING STARS. THOSE CLOUDS HAD NO WORRIES, NO FATHER YELLING AT HOME, NO BULLIES AT SCHOOL.

THEIR DESTINY WAS TO LIVE A PEACEFUL EXISTENCE, NEITHER AWARE NOR AGITATED, AND THEN FADE INTO THE DEPTH OF SPACE.

I TELL THIS STORY BECAUSE IT WAS THE LAST TIME I FELT A SENSE OF ORDER AND SERENITY IN MY LIFE BEFORE I FOUND THE TWELVE STEPS. I SLEPT WELL THAT NIGHT, AT PEACE THAT THE UNIVERSE HAD WRAPPED HER LOVING ARMS AROUND ME.

THEN MY DAD DIED.

TO ME IT WAS ALL SO SUDDEN, EVEN THOUGH I KNOW IT TOOK YEARS FOR THE BOOZE TO FINALLY GET HIM. SINCE MOM WAS A NURSE, I'M SURE SHE SAW MY DAD'S DECLINE THROUGH DIFFERENT EYES THAN MINE.

LOOKING BACK ON THIS, I KNOW NOW THAT DAD DIED OF CIRRHOSIS OF THE LIVER, ROTTING FROM THE INSIDE OUT. I WAS ONLY SIXTEEN WHEN HE DIED. FROM THAT POINT ON, I SWORE I WOULD NEVER TOUCH A DROP OF ALCOHOL.

THE THING ABOUT PARENTS IS THAT WE DON'T CHOOSE THEM. LIKE THE BIRTHMARK ON YOUR THIGH OR A MOLE BY YOUR NOSE, IT MIGHT NOT BE PRETTY, BUT IT'S WHAT YOU'RE GIVEN...

IT'S ALL YOU KNOW IN LIFE.

DAD'S ABSENCE WAS HARD TO GET USED TO.

I'D COME HOME FROM SCHOOL, OPEN THE DOOR, AND LOOK AT THAT PLAID RECLINER.

AND I WONDERED IF I REALLY EVER HAD A FATHER.

DAD NEVER HAD BEEN MUCH OF A BEER DRINKER.

HE LIKED HIS HARD DRINKS.

I THOUGHT TO MYSELF, "WHAT THE HELL, IT'S HOT OUT AND SO AM I, AND IT LOOKS GOOD."

WE'D DRIVE AROUND IN THE EVENINGS, AFTER WORK, AND EARL WOULD MAKE LEWD COMMENTS ABOUT GIRLS HE'D SEE. WITH EVERY CAN, EARL'S COMMENTS WOULD GET CRUDER. THE THING IS, AFTER FOUR OR FIVE BEERS CHUGGED DOWN ON AN EMPTY STOMACH, HIS REMARKS DIDN'T BOTHER ME. IT WAS FUN...OR SO I THOUGHT.

THAT GOT TO BE MY ROUTINE — ME AND EARL IN THE PICKUP, ROAD-TRIPPING AROUND THE LAKES IN MINNEAPOLIS OR OUT ON SOME RANDOM GRAVEL ROAD JUST OUTSIDE OF TOWN.

I FELT GROWN-UP. MOST OF ALL, I FELT IN CONTROL OF MY FEELINGS. "I'M NOT LIKE MY DAD," I THOUGHT.

IT'S ASTONISHING TO THINK THAT I WAS CONVINCED THAT BEER WASN'T ALCOHOL. YOU KNOW, THERE SHOULD HAVE BEEN LITTLE RED FLAGS THAT POPPED UP FOR ME, LIKE WHEN EARL THOUGHT IT WOULD BE A GOOD IDEA TO DRIVE ACROSS A BEACH NEXT TO A SWIMMING LAKE.

IT WASN'T FUNNY.

BUT I THOUGHT IT WAS.

THANK GOD NO ONE WAS HURT. WE DIDN'T END UP GETTING CAUGHT.

EARL WENT OFF TO COLLEGE IN THE FALL. MY GRADES WERE GOOD ENOUGH WHERE I COULD HAVE DONE THE SAME. AFTER DAD DIED, I HAD A SMALL NEST EGG HE LEFT FOR THE EXPRESS PURPOSE OF MY EDUCATION. BUT I WOULDN'T HAVE IT. DESPITE ALL MY MOTHER'S PLEADING FOR ME TO THINK OF MY FUTURE AND TO "BETTER MYSELF," I THOUGHT I KNEW WHAT I NEEDED.

SO THAT FALL IN '64 I APPLIED FOR A POSITION AT THE FORD PLANT WHERE MY OLD MAN HAD WORKED. IT WAS A STARTER JOB AT THE PLANT, AND IT WAS NOT FUN.

MY JOB WAS TO SORT ALL OF THE LITTLE ELECTRONIC DOODADS IN DIFFERENT COLORED BINS, AND GUYS CAME WITH PUSHCARTS TO MOVE THE BINS TO THE ASSEMBLY LINE.

IF I WAS DAYDREAMING...

...I LEARNED TO KEEP UP!

AFTER WORK, I'D DRIVE TO HUDSON, WISCONSIN...

...AND IT WASN'T TO TAKE IN WISCONSIN'S LEGENDARY CULTURE.

AT THAT TIME, MINNESOTA HAD A DRINKING AGE OF TWENTY-ONE. IN WISCONSIN, IT WAS EIGHTEEN — FOR BEER ONLY. THAT DIDN'T BOTHER ME...

I'M A BEER DRINKER...I LIKE MY BEER.

MOST OF THE TIME I'D HAVE A FEW ON THE WAY BACK TO MINNESOTA. LIFE WAS GOOD. WORK WAS DISAGREEABLE, BUT THAT WAS WORK. AFTER WORK IS WHERE LIFE REALLY WAS, I THOUGHT, DRIVING AROUND, HANGING OUT WITH MY FRIENDS FROM THE PLANT.

IT'S FUNNY THAT I FIRST STARTED DRINKING BEER BECAUSE IT LOOKED COLD AND DELICIOUS AND IT WOULD REFRESH ME ON THAT HOT DAY IN JULY. THEN I HAD BEER IN JANUARY. IT DIDN'T MATTER TO ME. I LIKED BEER AND IT LIKED ME.

AFTER A FEW I'D LOOSEN UP AND LIFE DIDN'T SEEM SO UNINTERESTING OR TENSE. JUST AS LONG AS I WASN'T DRINKING WHAT DAD DRANK, I DIDN'T CONSIDER IT DRINKING.

A QUESTION I GET FROM ALCOHOLICS AND NON-ALCOHOLICS ALIKE IS, WHEN DID I "BECOME" AN ALCOHOLIC?

WAS WHAT I WAS DOING AT NINETEEN IN 1965 **ABNORMAL**? WEREN'T OTHER YOUNG MEN AND WOMEN DOING EXACTLY THE SAME THING? HAD I PASSED A STAGE TO MY EVENTUAL DECAY? I HONESTLY DO NOT KNOW. BUT THAT'S JUST A TRIVIAL CURIOSITY IN THE PRESENT. IT IS NOT ESSENTIAL TO MY RECOVERY TO KNOW **WHEN** THE SHIFT **ACTUALLY HAPPENED** — JUST THAT **IT DID**.

I CAN ONLY LOOK AT THIS TIME AS EVIDENCE OF A DRUNK WHO WAS BEGINNING TO IMPROVE AT **DIGGING A DEEPER HOLE** FOR HIMSELF!

THE NEXT SUMMER I QUIT MY JOB AT FORD. EARL WAS HOME FROM COLLEGE. HE TOLD ME ABOUT A JOB IN CONSTRUCTION — THAT IT PAID WELL AND THAT IT WAS AWAY FROM HOME. THAT PART GRABBED MY ATTENTION. I WAS SICK OF LIVING AT MY MOM'S. I ASKED EARL WHERE THE JOB WAS, AND HE TOLD ME DULUTH, MINNESOTA. IT WAS ON LAKE SUPERIOR, NORTH OF MY HOME IN ST. PAUL.

THERE, I COULD MAKE MY OWN RULES, OR AT LEAST THE RULES THAT EARL AND I COULD LIVE BY...

29

EARLY IN THE MORNING TO THE LATE AFTERNOON WE WORKED LIKE SLAVES. I LIKED CONSTRUCTION. YOU COULD SEE AS THE DAY PROGRESSED WHAT YOU ACCOMPLISHED. AND I WAS GOOD AT IT. EARL HAD ANOTHER BUDDY FROM DULUTH WHO HAD A BOAT, AND WE'D TAKE TURNS DRUNK BOATING AROUND THE BAYS. BEER WAS EVER PRESENT. SO WAS SOMETHING NEW: MARIJUANA.

EARL HAD BEEN TO SCHOOL IN WASHINGTON STATE FOR HIS FRESHMAN YEAR. THERE, HE WAS INTRODUCED TO POT. ON A LAZY SATURDAY EVENING, I TOOK MY *FIRST HIT*. I DIDN'T CARE FOR IT. I GOT GIGGLY AND TOO DISORIENTED. I LIKED MY BOOZE; POT WAS TOO **DIFFERENT**.

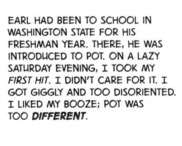

THAT'S THE THING, THOUGH...NONE OF US DID AN ACTIVITY FOR THE *ACTIVITY'S* SAKE ITSELF. **SOMETHING** HAD TO GO WITH IT — BEER, POT. EARL'S FRIEND JACK EVEN LIKED TO BRING A BOTTLE OF *ROT-GUT WHISKEY*, BUT I NEVER ASKED ABOUT *THAT*. I JUST SAW WHAT IT DID TO JACK: HE GOT **MEAN**, LIKE **MY DAD**.

THE NEXT TWO SUMMERS WE SPENT IN DULUTH, JUST THE THREE OF US, DRINKING AND RAISING HELL. IT WAS A FUN TIME, AND I STILL REMEMBER THOSE DAYS FONDLY. THAT'S AN ODD THING THAT I REMEMBER *THOSE* DAYS. I HAD *MANY MORE* **WORSE** DAYS DRINKING THAN I DID GOOD, BUT THOSE ARE THE DAYS I REMEMBER. THAT'S MY ALCOHOLIC BRAIN AT WORK, STILL, CHOOSING TO SEE **WHAT IT WANTS TO SEE.**

EVENTUALLY ALCOHOL DID FOR ME WHAT I DID NOT INTEND IT TO DO.

IT *PROGRESSED* INTO BECOMING THE *CENTER OF MY LIFE...*

...AND IT PROGRESSED TO *HARDER DRINK* TO GET ME THERE *QUICKER!*

I WAS SICK OF DULUTH. I WANTED A NEW PLACE TO PARTY. AND THE TOWN, ESPECIALLY IN THE WINTER, WAS BEGINNING TO WEAR THIN.

WHAT TO DO FOR A YOUNG MAN WHO LIVES IN HIS HEAD TOO MUCH, WANTS CONSTANT STIMULATION OR GETS EASILY BORED, AND IS ESSENTIALLY SELF-FOCUSED ABOUT WHAT LIFE *SHOULD GIVE HIM*?

31

BOOT CAMP WAS *HARD*. IT TOOK AWAY ALL THAT WAS *IMMATURE* IN ME.

BUT EVEN THE *ARMY* COULDN'T TAKE AWAY MY *ALCOHOLISM*!

I WAS ASSIGNED TO A BASE CAMP ON THE BONG SON PLAIN IN SOUTH VIETNAM. MY PLATOON WAS THE FORWARD OBSERVER AND RECON UNIT FOR THE ARTILLERY, THE BIG GUNS. REMEMBER WHEN I TOLD YOU THAT I THOUGHT MY VOLUNTARY ENLISTMENT WOULD GIVE ME SPECIAL TREATMENT? IT DID. THE POWERS-THAT-BE DECIDED THAT MY GIFTS WERE IN CALLING THE SHOTS OF THE BIG GUNS. I WOULD HAVE RATHER BEEN BEHIND THE BIG GUNS, TENS OF MILES AWAY FROM THE ENEMY.

INSTEAD, I WAS A "HIGH-PRIORITY TARGET" OF THE VIET CONG.

FORWARD OBSERVERS WERE SO *HATED* BY THE ENEMY BECAUSE THEY WERE GIVEN THE POWER TO DIRECT *ENORMOUS FIREPOWER* AGAINST THEM! KILLING *YOU* TAKES AWAY THE *EYES* OF THE BIG GUNS. SO MY DREAM OF FINDING PURPOSE AND MEANING — AND SETTLING MY CONSTANT AGITATION — *INSTEAD*...

...GAVE ME A NEW REASON TO LIVE SCARED.

I THOUGHT I WAS LUCKY, THOUGH...

...BECAUSE WARTIME GAVE ME THE OPPORTUNITY TO DRINK AGAIN.

IT'S FUNNY; THE MILITARY DIDN'T WANT YOU TO DRINK IN BASIC, BUT THEY DIDN'T SEEM TO GIVE A SHIT WHEN YOU WERE FIGHTING. OF COURSE, OUR COMMANDING OFFICERS WOULDN'T LET US DRINK OUT IN THE FIELD, BUT IN THE DOWN-TIME — *AND WE HAD A LOT* — A GUY COULD FIND BEER, HASH, EVEN HEROIN. EVERYONE SEEMED TO BE DOING *SOMETHING*.

I REMEMBER THINKING, "HOLY SHIT — I'M BECOMING *MY DAD!*"

IT DIDN'T SEEM TO FAZE ME ALL THAT MUCH. THAT'S HOW IT IS, ISN'T IT? YOU DO SOMETHING YOU TOLD YOURSELF *YOU'D NEVER DO* AND *YOU GET USED TO IT.* ALCOHOL IS *CUNNING, BAFFLING,* **POWERFUL**! AND *ALCOHOL-ISM* IS *CREEPING,* **DEVIOUS**!

THE TERROR OF THE WAR WAS SOON OVER FOR ME, THOUGH.

WE HAD A MISSION TO SPOT FOR INDIRECT FIRE COVERING AN INFANTRY ASSAULT TO A *HEAVILY FORTIFIED HILL* CALLED **DONG AP BIA**. THE BATTLE BECAME KNOWN AS THE **BATTLE FOR HAMBURGER HILL**, MOSTLY BECAUSE GUYS TURNED INTO HAMBURGER AFTER EVERY FRONTAL ASSAULT.

FOR TEN DAYS, DOZENS AND DOZENS OF MEN LOST THEIR LIVES OVER A POINT ON A MAP THAT HAD **NO STRATEGIC VALUE**. I BEGAN TO BECOME CYNICAL ABOUT THE WAR.

TO TOP IT OFF, IT WAS MAY, THE RAINY SEASON.

I WAS ALSO DRUNK MOST OF THE BATTLE. IT'S UNBELIEVABLE, I KNOW... BUT I HAD GOTTEN MYSELF SEVERAL BOTTLES OF WHISKEY...

...AND WAS ABLE TO KEEP THEM TO MYSELF.

I WAS PERCHED IN FULL CAMO IN A **STRANGLER FIG** TREE. WE LOVED THOSE TREES BECAUSE THEY WERE EASY TO CLIMB AND THEY CONCEALED YOU WELL. I HAD MY RADIO, MY BINOCS, MY GUN, AND — OF COURSE — **A BOTTLE**.

MY RADIO LAY ON MY LAP AND FROM TIME TO TIME ORDERS BARKED FROM IT, DEMANDING PRECISE CALCULATIONS OF DISTANCE AND AREA FOR ARTILLERY FIRE. AT THIS POINT I DIDN'T CARE ABOUT ANYTHING OR ANYBODY BUT MYSELF. I'M SURE THAT MY CALCULATIONS WERE OFF AT THIS POINT. IT'S A MIRACLE NO ONE ON OUR SIDE WAS KILLED BY MISDIRECTION.

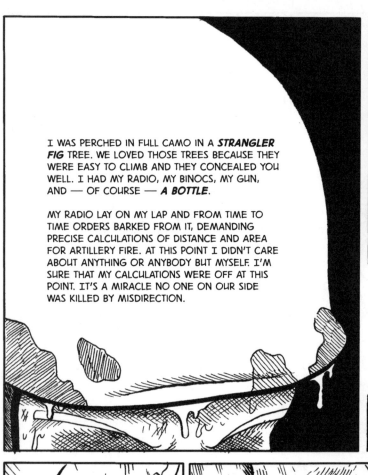

I SAT, CONCEALED IN MY PRIVATE TREE-HAMMOCK, WITH THE ALCOHOLIC HAZE DIMMING THE HIDEOUS EVIL THAT MEN DO TO EACH OTHER. BUT, THE NEXT THING I KNEW...

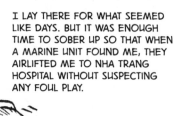

I LAY THERE FOR WHAT SEEMED LIKE DAYS. BUT IT WAS ENOUGH TIME TO SOBER UP SO THAT WHEN A MARINE UNIT FOUND ME, THEY AIRLIFTED ME TO NHA TRANG HOSPITAL WITHOUT SUSPECTING ANY FOUL PLAY.

THUNK!

I HAD TO FINISH MY TOUR WITH OFFICE DUTIES IN A STUFFY, DIMLY LIT ROOM AT THE REDSTONE ARSENAL IN NORTHERN ALABAMA. IF FIGHTING THE WAR IN VIETNAM DIDN'T MAKE ME CYNICAL, FILING GOVERNMENT DOCUMENTS AT THE REDSTONE TECHNICAL TEST CENTER DID. I GOT AN **HONORABLE DISCHARGE** FROM THE ARMY IN THE FALL OF 1970.

AND LET ME TELL YOU...

I'M NOT PROUD AT ALL FOR GETTING THAT HONORABLE DISCHARGE. THERE WAS NOTHIN' HONORABLE ABOUT IT.

ST. PAUL
POP. 309,980

AFTER MY DISCHARGE, I DECIDED TO RETURN TO MY ROOTS.

AND...I THOUGHT I'D LOOK UP MY BEST DRINKING BUDDY, EARL.

BUT...

37

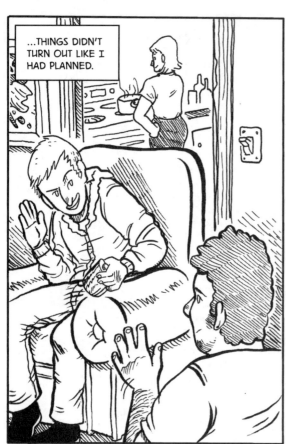

...THINGS DIDN'T TURN OUT LIKE I HAD PLANNED.

IT DISAPPOINTED ME THAT EARL WASN'T GOING DRINKING WITH ME.

IT'S SAD TO THINK THAT ALCOHOL WAS *MORE OF A FRIEND* TO ME AT THAT TIME *THAN **HE WAS***.

I TOLD EARL SOME OF MY SANITIZED STORIES ABOUT THE WAR AND MADE SMALL TALK WITH HIS FAMILY BEFORE I LEFT...I HEADED IMMEDIATELY TO A PARK AND WENT TO A PLACE WITH MY *"BEST FRIEND."*

WELL, I GOT A JOB. A CONSTRUCTION JOB. I WORKED MY WAY UP. BUT THE WHOLE TIME I KEPT MY "BEST FRIEND" WITH ME.

I THOUGHT I WAS IN CONTROL, AND I GAVE ALL SORTS OF EXCUSES *TO MYSELF*!

"ALL HARD-WORKING GUYS LIKE TO DRINK."

"OTHER PEOPLE MIGHT NOT BE ABLE TO DRINK ON THE JOB, BUT I CAN HANDLE IT."

"SLEEP COMES SO MUCH EASIER WHEN I HAVE A NIGHTCAP."

"I'M A GREAT GUY WHEN I DRINK!"

"I'M FUNNIER."

"I'M MORE AT EASE."

"IT'S THE *REAL ME.*"

38

AND THAT'S THE THING ABOUT MY ALCOHOL USE:

FOR A WHILE I THOUGHT I WAS *MANAGING IT*.

THAT'S NOT *REALLY* THE WAY IT WAS: IT WAS *MANAGING ME*.

2-FOR-1

SMOOTH BOURBON ALWAYS SATISFIES

I WOULD COME TO LEARN THAT MY ADDICTION WOULD, IN DUE COURSE, *DEMAND* PRIORITY OVER *EVERYTHING*, EVEN THE WOMAN I MARRIED.

ON MY TWENTY-SIXTH BIRTHDAY, MY MOM AND MY BROTHER PAUL AND HIS WIFE, KATE, TOOK ME OUT FOR STEAK.

A YOUNG, BLONDE WOMAN CARRYING A PAD OF PAPER APPROACHED OUR TABLE. THE WAITRESS LOOKED AT ME, SMILED, AND I SAW THEM...

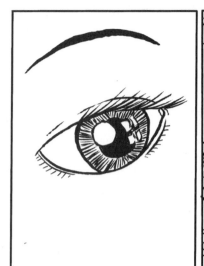

SHE HAD...

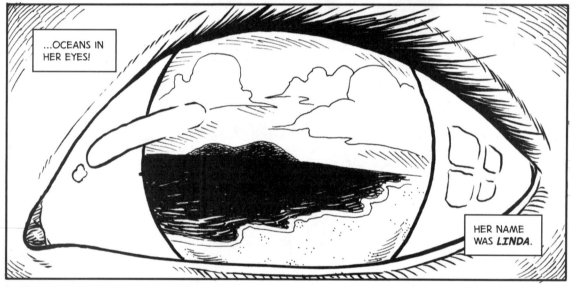
...OCEANS IN HER EYES!

HER NAME WAS *LINDA*.

MY PURSUIT OF LINDA WAS AWKWARD. THE BEST PLAN I HAD WAS TO EAT AT THAT PLACE AS OFTEN AS I COULD. WHEN LINDA WAS THERE, I'D LEAVE A BIG TIP.

WHEN SHE WASN'T, I DIDN'T. OF COURSE, I ALWAYS HAD PLENTY OF DRINKS TOO.

SHE GREW TO LOVE ME AND I LOVED HER. LINDA GAVE ME THE GIFT OF SEEING MYSELF DIFFERENTLY. SHE SAW A MAN WITH DEPTH OF EMOTION AND AN ACHING PULL TO FIND LIFE'S MEANING AND PURPOSE. I SUPPOSE MY "FUNCTIONAL ALCOHOLISM" WAS HIDDEN ENOUGH AT THIS TIME. MAYBE SHE DIDN'T KNOW.

I DO!

LINDA WAS PLAYFULLY INTELLIGENT. UNLIKE ME, SHE HAD GONE TO COLLEGE. UNLIKE ME, SHE CAME FROM A STABLE FAMILY. EVEN WITH OUR DIFFERENCES, WE BELONGED TOGETHER.

AFTER LINDA HAD FINISHED HER SUMMER JOB AT THE RESTAURANT, SHE TOOK THE CPA EXAM AND BECAME A JUNIOR PARTNER IN AN ACCOUNTING FIRM.

SHE HAD MANY INTERESTS: SHE PLAYED THE PIPE ORGAN AT HER CHURCH; SHE LOVED TO GARDEN; BOOKS WERE EVERYWHERE IN HER APARTMENT; SHE LOVED TO COOK. LINDA WAS AN AMAZING HUMAN BEING, AND SHE WAS MINE. I WAS HAPPIER THAN I'D BEEN IN A LONG TIME.

I SHOULD HAVE STAYED HAPPY. I THOUGHT I FELT HAPPINESS IN FLEETING INTERVALS, BUT I FOUND MYSELF YEARNING FOR MORE.

I QUIT THE JOB I HAD GOTTEN AFTER THE WAR. THE BOSS WAS STARTING TO GET SUSPICIOUS THAT I WAS NIPPING ON THE JOB, WHICH I WAS. STILL, HE GAVE A GOOD RECOMMENDATION TO ANOTHER FIRM, WHICH BUILT OFFICE BUILDINGS.

IT WAS SOMETHING I HAD NEVER DONE BEFORE. BUT MY EXPERIENCE AND MY WILLINGNESS TO WORK HARD PAID OFF AND I SOON BECAME AN ASSISTANT CONTRACTOR FOR THE FIRM.

MY JOB WAS TO WORK WITH ARCHITECTS AND ENGINEERS TO ORDER APPROPRIATE MATERIALS FOR THE CONSTRUCTION. I FELT LIKE I *HAD IT ALL*. BUT I STILL WANTED *MORE*...

BUT, HONESTLY, IT DIDN'T MATTER HOW SMART I THOUGHT I WAS. IN LIFE I WAS FLAILING ABOUT, BECAUSE MY *LOVE AFFAIR* WITH *ALCOHOL* WAS BECOMING *UNMANAGEABLE*.

DURING THIS TIME, LINDA BEGAN TO NOTICE MY PATTERN OF DRINKING: THAT ON SATURDAY MORNINGS, SHE MIGHT AS WELL NOT TALK TO ME, SINCE I WOULD BE NURSING A HANG-OVER; SHE SAW HOW EVENINGS WERE FILLED WITH A BEER AND A BOOK (ALTHOUGH MY HABIT OF READING BECAME LESS AS I DRANK MORE AND I OPTED FOR STUPID SITCOMS IN PLACE OF READING); AND SHE FOUND A FLASK IN MY JACKET MORE THAN ONCE.

THERE WERE ACCUSATIONS...

I HAD PLENTY OF EXCUSES...

AS LINDA TOLERATED MY DRINKING LESS, SHE BECAME MORE VOCAL. INSTEAD OF CUTTING BACK OR QUITTING, I BEGAN TO HIDE MY HABIT IN NEW, CREATIVE WAYS.

WE'VE ALL GOT OUR HIDING PLACES, DON'T WE?

43

BY THE TIME WE HAD TRACY, OUR *BABY GIRL*, I WAS BROODING OVER MY USE.

I STILL DENIED THAT I HAD BECOME MY FATHER. IN SOME WAYS, *I WASN'T ONE.*

I BEGAN TO WITHDRAW AND *LIVE IN MY HEAD.* THIS IS SOMETHING THAT *ALL ALCOHOLICS — AND I'D ADD, ADDICTS TOO — SUFFER FROM.* WE GOT THE HAMSTER RUNNING IN A WHEEL UP IN OUR HEADS...

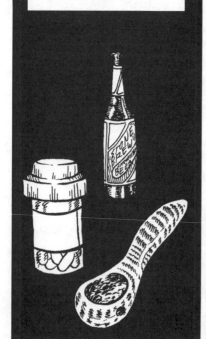

...AND WITHOUT THE *TWELVE STEPS*, WE ALWAYS GO BACK TO DOING WHAT WE DO BEST, TO TRY TO SLOW THAT OL' HAMSTER DOWN.

ONE DAY, LINDA WENT TO CHOIR PRACTICE AT CHURCH. I WAS TAKING CARE OF TRACY. SHE WOULDN'T STOP FUSSING. "LIFE ISN'T FAIR," I THOUGHT. WITH EVERY BURST OF TRACY'S CRYING I LOOKED AT THE CEILING, BEHIND WHICH WAS AN ABSENT, UNCARING GOD, LIGHT-YEARS AWAY FROM MY SUFFERING. *WHY CAN'T MY BABY GIRL SHUT UP?* IT WAS ALL ABOUT ME, *GODDAMMIT!*

45

I CAN SAFELY SAY THAT THE HELL I WENT THROUGH THAT MORNING WAS CLOSE TO THE HELL I ENCOUNTERED IN WAR, WITH ONE VITAL DIFFERENCE: THE BULLETS FIRED AT ME NOW WERE COMING FROM SOMEONE WHO I SUPPOSEDLY LOVED.

AND TO THINK THAT I TRUSTED YOU. YOU SAID YOU WEREN'T GOING TO DRINK, LARRY! FOR GOD'S SAKE, IT'S OUR DAUGHTER!

THEN, I SAW THE REAL PROBLEM FOR WHAT IT WAS... ...THERE SEEMED TO BE *NO SOLUTION*.

THIS CAN'T GO ON

I CAN'T STOP

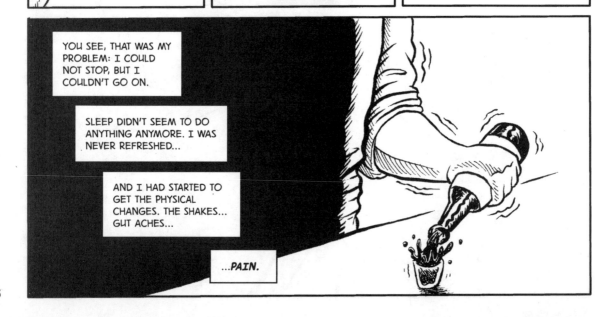

YOU SEE, THAT WAS MY PROBLEM: I COULD NOT STOP, BUT I COULDN'T GO ON.

SLEEP DIDN'T SEEM TO DO ANYTHING ANYMORE. I WAS NEVER REFRESHED...

AND I HAD STARTED TO GET THE PHYSICAL CHANGES. THE SHAKES... GUT ACHES...

...*PAIN.*

ANY **NORMAL** PERSON SEEING MY LIFE WOULD RESPOND THE SAME AS LINDA HAD.

YOUR **LIFE** — IT'S **INSANE!**

MY FALL FROM THIS IVORY PILLAR OF GLORY FINALLY CAME WHEN I WAS THIRTY-FOUR YEARS OLD. DESPITE MY BEST EFFORTS TO CONTROL MY USAGE, THE PIPER RETURNED AND HE WANTED *PAYMENT*. IN *FULL*. WITH **INTEREST**.

THE DAY THE COUNTY SHERIFF'S DEPART-MENT INTERVENED FOR ME WAS NOT FUN. BUT IT WAS SOMETHING I BELIEVE **HAD TO HAPPEN** TO SHAKE MY UNDER-STANDING OF LIFE. I HAVE NOTHING BUT GOODWILL FOR THE MEN AND WOMEN WHO SERVE IN LAW ENFORCEMENT. THEY PUT THEIR LIVES ON THE LINE TO MAKE SURE THAT OTHERS ARE PROTECTED. I BELIEVE **MY HIGHER POWER WAS WORKING THROUGH THEM** WHEN THEY ARRESTED ME.

IT WAS WHEN I WAS **THIRTY-FOUR**. I'D STARTED THAT MORNING LIKE MOST OF THE MORNINGS — WITH PLENTY TO DRINK, RIGHT IN THE CAR. I GUESS I HAD MORE THAN I THOUGHT. ON THE WAY TO A CONSTRUCTION SITE, I HAD TO PASS THE STATE CAPITOL BUILDING. I'D BEEN BY THERE A THOUSAND TIMES, AND I KNOW TO SLOW DOWN BY THE HILL ON THE FAR SIDE. BUT, I DIDN'T. AND, I WAS *TOO DRUNK*. I SLAMMED RIGHT INTO OUR **STATE CAPITOL BUILDING**!

WHAT HAPPENED NEXT WASN'T FUN. AND, TO BE HONEST, I DON'T REMEMBER A LOT OF IT. I SPENT A COUPLE OF WEEKS IN LOCKUP. OF COURSE, I HAD TO PAY FOR THE DAMAGE TO THE CAPITOL BUILDING. MIRACULOUSLY, IN IT ALL, LINDA STAYED WITH ME. THAT WAS A HUGE GIFT. I GOT ANOTHER GIFT TOO...

IT WASN'T EASY FOR ME AT FIRST. IT SEEMED SO *STRANGE*, SO *FOREIGN*...

HI. MY NAME IS DREW. I'M AN ALCOHOLIC.

HI, DREW.

...BUT IT ALL GOT EASIER, ONCE I OPENED UP AND LET THE PROGRAM WORK.

HEY THERE. YOU SAID YOUR NAME WAS LARRY?

I'M CONNOR. SAY, DO YOU HAVE A SPONSOR YET?

CONNOR BECAME MY SPONSOR IN AA. OVER THAT FIRST YEAR I WOULD LEARN THE *TWELVE STEPS*. MORE IMPORTANTLY, CONNOR SHARED HIS STORY WITH ME AND GUIDED ME. AND, YOU KNOW WHAT? IT WASN'T EASY. I WON'T LIE TO YOU — THERE ARE TIMES WHEN I'VE STRUGGLED. BUT HERE'S WHAT I KNOW NOW: THE *TWELVE STEPS* MOVED ME OUT OF A WORLD OF *SERVING MYSELF* INTO A NEW ONE OF *SERVING OTHERS*.

AND *THAT*, MY FRIENDS, IS MY STORY. WHY DON'T WE ALL STAND AND SHARE THE SERENITY PRAYER TO CLOSE THIS MEETING?

CLAP!
CLAP!
CLAP!
CLAP!
CLAP!
CLAP!

MEANWHILE...

WHOA! WHAT THE...?!

HOW THE...? SPENCER, HOW'D WE GET IN *LONDON*? AND ON TOP OF **BIG BEN** FOR THAT MATTER?!

OH...I GET IT. WE'RE HERE TO SHOW YOU SOMETHING!

THERE'S NOTHING QUITE LIKE *GETTING HIGH*. ISN'T THAT RIGHT?

THAT'S SOME-THING THAT NON-ADDICTS DON'T UNDERSTAND.

OTHERS DON'T GET HOW *FUN* IT IS TO GET *DRUNK* OR *HIGH* OR HOW IT MAKES LIVING *WITHIN OUR OWN SKIN* **BEARABLE**!

PROBLEM IS...

51

53

UM...HI.
UH, SIR? I HAVE A
QUESTION FOR
YOU.

HA
HA HA

HA
HA
HA

NO!
WAIT...

WHAT'S
YOUR
NAME?

I'M
HANNAH.

WELL, HANNAH...
WELCOME. I'M LARRY. I
WASN'T LAUGHING AT YOU.
IT'S JUST THAT I'M NOT
USED TO BEING CALLED
"SIR." ESPECIALLY IN A
MEETING...

IN A MEETING, WE'RE ALL THE *SAME*. WE'RE *ADDICTS* AND *ALCOHOLICS*, PLAIN AND SIMPLE.

WHAT WOULD YOU LIKE TO ASK?

OKAY, I'LL JUST SAY IT: I DON'T THINK I'M LIKE YOU. WHY *SHOULDN'T* I GET HIGH IF I WANT?

THERE ISN'T ANY REASON YOU SHOULDN'T.

AND, WHO ARE YOU? YOU'RE FROM THE UK, RIGHT?

ALEX. AND...YEAH, I'M FROM LONDON — *EAST END*. YOU KNOW WHAT THAT MEANS?

YEAH. I KNOW WHAT THAT MEANS. IT MEANS YOU'RE FROM *THE SHIT*.

HA-HA! THAT'S RIGHT. SHE'S A CLEVER ONE, INNIT?

UH, BUT YOU DIDN'T ANSWER MY QUESTION. WHY SHOULDN'T I GET HIGH? I *LIKE* IT.

BUT THAT'S THE THING. *YOU CAN*. SOON ENOUGH — IF YOU'RE TRUTHFUL — YOU'LL KNOW YOU'RE NOT MAN-AGING IT. IT'S *MANAGING YOU!*

LEMME TELL YOU SOMETHIN'...I KNOW YOU CAN RELATE, *HANNAH-GIRL*...

I WAS BORN IN LONDON IN THE EAST END. HANNAH, YOU'RE RIGHT. IT'S THE SHIT. AND THAT DOESN'T MEAN IT'S GREAT. NOT WITH US. NO WAY. IT IS A BIT...*ROUGH*.

MY GRANDPARENTS WERE FROM GHANA IN AFRICA. THEY CAME TO ENGLAND DURING THE FIRST WORLD WAR. MY GRANDFATHER WAS A SAILOR, A HAND ON THE DOCKS. HE WORKED HIMSELF TO DEATH SO MY MUM HAD A LIFE. WHEN I WAS LITTLE, NOT A DAY PASSED WHERE SHE FAILED TO TELL ME TO RESPECT MY GRANDFATHER.

BUT MY LIFE WAS DIFFICULT STILL. MY DAD, YOU KNOW HOW IT IS...HARD DRINKER, POVERTY, YOU KNOW WHAT I MEAN...HE WASN'T THERE. BUT THAT WASN'T A PROBLEM. OTHER GUYS WERE THERE.

GROWING UP BLACK IN ENGLAND IS DIF-
FERENT THAN IT IS IN AMERICA. WE HAVE A
DIFFERENT HISTORY. BUT OUR CLASS
SYSTEM IS STRICTER. I WASN'T ON TOP,
NOT AT ALL. STOP 'N' SEARCH ALL THE
TIME. THAT GOT BETTER LATER, WHEN WE
KNEW HOW TO HANDLE THE LAW.

THE OLDER BOYS WERE MY FATHER
FIGURES. THEY FILLED IN WHERE
MY OWN DAD WAS ABSENT. WE
WERE TOGETHER ALL THE TIME.

AS I GREW UP IN THE ESTATES —
Y'KNOW THAT'S LIKE YOUR "PROJECTS"
— I'D SKIP SCHOOL MORE AND
MORE. MY MUM HATED IT. SHE SAID
I DISRESPECTED MY GRANDDAD. ALL
I KNEW WAS THAT MY BOYS CARED
ABOUT ME AND THAT THEY WERE FUN.
SUCCESSFUL TOO. THEY HAD MONEY
AND INFLUENCE. WHAT DID I HAVE?
WHAT COULD I DO?

LIKE I SAID, IT WASN'T A
GANG. BUT THERE WERE
GANGS. MOSTLY ASIAN ONES.
AND WE HAD TO DEFEND OUR
BUSINESS. I DID THIS AS A
KID. IT WAS THE LATE '90S.

OH YES, OUR BUSINESS...
WE SOLD "*FINE PRODUCTS*" TO
OUR CUSTOMERS. EVERY BLOCK OF
FLATS HAD BUYERS, USERS. I
STARTED SELLING SKUNK, WEED.

WE GOT THE STRONGER STUFF
SOONER THAN YOU AMERICANS.
THE POLICE USUALLY KEPT OUT OF
OUR BUSINESS; THEY COULDN'T BE
BOTHERED WITH US.

I SMOKED TOO. EVERYONE —
ALL MY BOYS DID IT. IT WAS
NORMAL. IT WAS MY LIFE.
EVERY DAY...

I QUIT SCHOOL. I LEFT HOME.
BROKE MY MUM'S HEART TOO. I
SET MYSELF UP, STARTED SELLING
FULL TIME. ME AND MY MATES,
WE WERE SAFE. LIFE WAS GOOD.

THE TIME CAME WHEN WE WANTED TO MOVE UP, SO TO SPEAK. YOU KNOW, GET OUT OF THE EAST END AND SCORE SOME REAL MONEY.

A FRIEND OF MY MATES KNEW A GUY FROM THE NETHERLANDS, A CHEMIST. THIS GUY COOKED UP X. FINE AS IT COMES. YOU YANKS CALL HER **MOLLY**. TO US, SHE WAS **MANDY**. ALL THE SAME, SHE WAS PURE CANDY AND SHE **MADE** US...

SHE MADE US RICH, THAT IS.

WE DISCOVERED THE LONDON CLUB SCENE, WHICH IS *INTENSE* AND BRIMMING FULL OF KIDS WITH **MONEY** TO **GET HIGH.**

FIRST, WE SOLD TO THE **YOUNGERS**. THAT WAS DANGEROUS, THOUGH. TOO MANY EYES SAW OUR FACES. WE DIDN'T LIKE THAT.

OUR CONNECTION WITH THE DUTCHMAN SUPPLIED US MONTHLY, SO WE MOVED TO SELLING ONLY TO MIDDLEMEN, WHO SOLD TO THE YOUNGERS, THE RAVERS. FEWER FACES MEANT LESS POTENTIAL SNITCHES. WE WERE FLUSH. AND WE LIVED IT UP.

THING IS, IT WASN'T **REALLY LIVING**, BUT I WOULDN'T FIND THIS OUT UNTIL **LATER.**

WE SPENT MOST DAYS TRADING WITH OUR SELLERS. WE PREFERRED TO DO THIS IN THE DAY, IN THE LATE MORNING, ONLY IN PLACES OF OUR CHOOSING.

FINISH 'EM!!

EVENINGS, OUR SCHEDULE WAS FREE. WE'D SMOKE. PLAY. EAT. EAT SOME MORE!

OR WE'D HEAD TO THE CLUBS.

ONE NIGHT, WE HIT OUR SPECIAL STASH OF *MANDY*. WE SMOKED A LOT OF BUD, BUT UP TO THAT POINT, WE HADN'T DROPPED ANY OF OUR SUPPLY OF X. YOU ALWAYS REMEMBER YOUR VIRGIN HIT, RIGHT?

THAT NIGHT WAS KICKIN', MAN!

IF YOU DON'T OVERHEAT AND DIE, OR TAKE SO MUCH THAT YOUR SEROTONIN RECEPTORS FRY IN YOUR BRAIN, ECSTASY BRINGS YOU TO A PLACE YOU NEVER WANT TO LEAVE. BUT, *THAT'S THE RUB*...

YOU NEVER GET BACK TO THAT PLACE, *EVER AGAIN*!

IT'S RUBBISH. SHIT, REALLY. BUT THAT'S WHERE *MANDY* TOOK ME: TO HEAVEN, ONCE. THEN, I CHASED HER FOREVER, NEVER TO FIND 'ER AGAIN!

FIND ME!

THAT'S HOW IT WAS TWO, THREE TIMES A WEEK FOR *SIX* YEARS!

MY LOVE WAS *X*. BUT SHE DIDN'T LOVE ME LIKE SHE HAD THAT FIRST TIME. IT'S ABSOLUTELY INSANE THAT I COULD BE SO *DAFT* AS TO NOT SEE WHAT WAS HAPPENING TO ME: I WAS *CHANGING THE WIRING* IN MY BRAIN!

WE WERE MAKING SO MUCH MONEY, I NEVER ONCE LOOKED TO MY FUTURE. I THOUGHT IT WOULD GO ON FOREVER. BUT, THINGS WENT DOWN-HILL AFTER THAT, AS THEY *ALWAYS* DO.

AT FIRST, I THOUGHT THINGS WERE GET-TING BETTER.

I MET SOMEONE.

IT WAS SOMEONE WHO WAS VERY SPECIAL TO ME.

HIS NAME WAS *CHARLIE*. I LOVED HIM WITH ALL MY HEART.

ER...AHEM...
YES, HANNAH-GIRL.
I'M GAY.

BUT, HERE'S THE THING: *IT DOESN'T MATTER.* **IT DOESN'T MATTER AT ALL** WHERE YOU COME FROM — WHETHER YOU'RE STRAIGHT OR GAY, A WOMAN OR A MAN, FROM LONDON OR FROM SOUTH FLORIDA, NOT IF YOU'RE BLACK OR WHITE OR...**WHOEVER YOU ARE**. IF YOU'RE AN ADDICT OR AN ALCOHOLIC, **THAT'S WHO YOU ARE.**

IT TOOK ME A SPELL TO SORT THAT OUT FOR MYSELF, THOUGH. *AND IT COST...*

BEVERAGES--

IT COST—
SORRY...

IT COST ME
DEARLY.

CHARLIE WORKED IN THE CITY. IN BANKING.

HE KNEW WHAT I DID. IT DIDN'T SEEM TO BOTHER HIM MUCH.

AND MY BOYS WERE COOL WITH HIM. SO IT ALL LOOKED GOOD. UNTIL...

YOU SEE, CHARLIE LIKED TO PARTY. *HARD.*

HE LOVED ECSTASY EVEN MORE THAN I DID. AND *THAT* IS SAYING A LOT.

X STARTED TO TAKE ITS TOLL ON CHARLIE. THE SHIVERS...

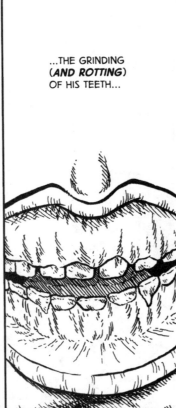

...THE GRINDING (*AND ROTTING*) OF HIS TEETH...

...THE DEPRESSION.

AND THERE WERE SEVERAL TRIPS TO *A & E* — THE ER. CLOSE CALLS, THEY WERE.

MERGENCY

IT'S NOT LIKE I WASN'T BEING AFFECTED TOO BY X. AFTER ALL, I WAS *AN ADDICT*. BY THIS TIME, I HAD TO TAKE IT JUST TO *FEEL NORMAL*. BUT, WITH CHARLIE, IT JUST SEEMED TO HIT HIM *PHYSICALLY* HARDER THAN ME.

AND, ONE MORNING, AFTER A NIGHT OF PARTYING...

THE UNTHINKABLE!!

TURNS OUT THE X ISN'T WHAT KILLED HIM. IT WAS THE COMEDOWN DRUGS — *BENZOS*. HE JUST WANTED TO SLEEP; HE WANTED TO CHILL. HE TOOK A HANDFUL, AND HE GOT THE REST HE WANTED — *PERMANENTLY*. THE NEXT WEEKS WERE *MAJOR STRESS*. I COULDN'T PARTY, SO I DIDN'T HAVE ANY X. I WAS *GUTTED*. I WANTED THE PAIN TO STOP. I WANTED TO DIE.

SO, I GOT SOME "SUPPLIES." HEROIN.

I HAD HIT OPIATES BEFORE. I LIKED THEM, BUT THEY WEREN'T AS GOOD AS ECSTASY FOR ME. I KNEW HOW MUCH WOULD GET ME HIGH, AND I KNEW HOW MUCH WOULD GIVE ME THE *FINAL REST* I DESPERATELY WANTED. AND I GOT IT...

...*ALMOST.*

TURNS OUT ONE OF MY BOYS FOUND ME OD'ING, PASSED OUT ON THE FLOOR. HE RALLIED THE REST OF MY MATES TO DRIVE ME TO THE FRONT OF A HOSPITAL DOOR AND PUSH MY UNCONSCIOUS BODY OUT ON THE GROUND. THEY DIDN'T EVEN BOTHER TO STAY. YES, THOSE WERE MY "FRIENDS," MY "MATES."

THE NEXT FOUR WEEKS WEREN'T FUN...

...BUT BEING IN *REHAB* — A ***GOVERNMENT-SPONSORED REHAB***, NO LESS — IS NO EASY RIDE. GRADUALLY, THOUGH, I BEGAN TO NOTICE JUST HOW ***UNMANAGEABLE*** MY LIFE HAD BECOME. IT WAS A CAROUSEL (WHAT DO YOU AMERICANS CALL IT? A ***MERRY-GO-ROUND***?). I COULDN'T EVER GET OFF. I WAS ALWAYS CHASING. ALWAYS WANTING. ALWAYS TRYING TO GET SOMEWHERE I NEVER WOULD, BECAUSE I WAS ***GOING IN CIRCLES***!

AND, DAVID, MY COUNSELOR, TAUGHT ME THAT THE ***TWELVE STEPS*** START WITH ***STEP ONE*** FOR A REASON.

DAVID WAS A GUY WHO LISTENED — ***REALLY LISTENED*** — TO ME. HE WAS IN RECOVERY HIMSELF. AND HE LET ME SEE THE TRUTH OF MY LIFE: THAT IT HAD ***SPUN OUT OF CONTROL*** AND WAS ***INSANE***. I DIDN'T WANT TO DIE. I'M A RATIONAL BLOKE IN MY HEAD (AND MY HEART). SO...I LISTENED.

NA (NARCOTICS ANONYMOUS) WAS MY THING. NOTHING AGAINST AA — AFTER ALL, ALCOHOL IS A DRUG TOO. BOTH GROUPS ARE TWELVE STEP BASED.

NOW, I'VE LEFT ***THAT LIFE***. I'M SELLING ***FINE AUTOMOBILES IN LONDON***, AND I'M HAPPIER THAN EVER.

BUT I MAKE *AT LEAST* FIVE MEETINGS A WEEK. ***I HAVE TO!***

I OWE MY LIFE TODAY TO THE ***NA STEP*** THAT STARTED IT ALL FOR ME:

STEP ONE
"We admitted that we were powerless over our addiction, that our lives had become unmanageable."

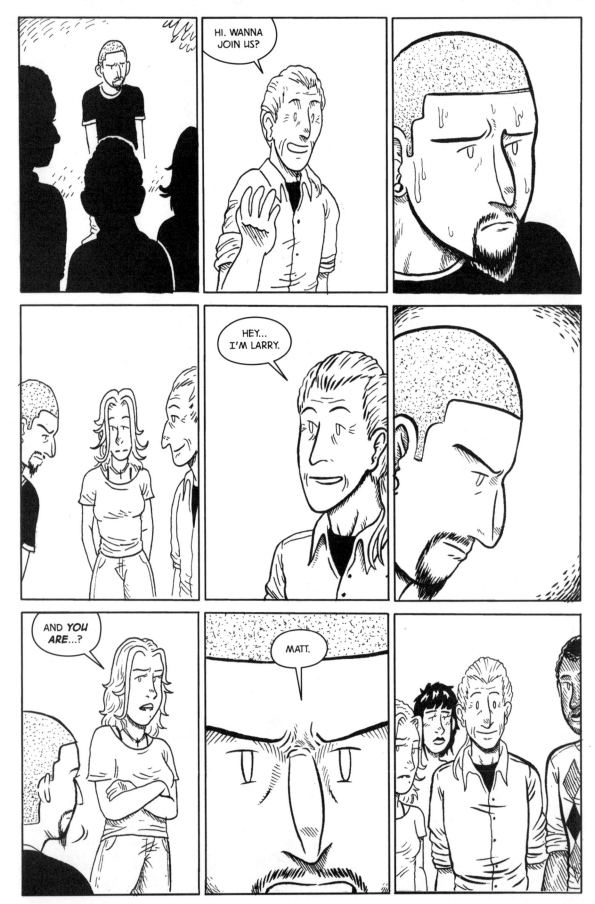

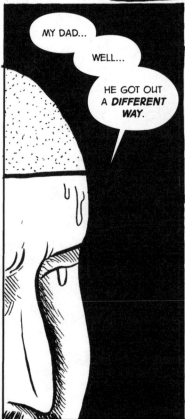

74

THAT'S RIGHT. MY DAD GOT **ALL RELIGIOUS** ON US. HE GOT OUTTA THE GANG.

MY POPS STARTED WORKIN' AT THE DOCKS AT **DAYGO**. THEY GOT THOSE BIG CRUISE SHIPS THERE. HE LOADED THE SUPPLIES.

XAVIER

BUT, PRETTY SOON, HE WORKED HIS WAY UP. BY THE TIME I WAS THREE, MY POPS ENDED UP BUYING A COMPANY THAT SUPPLIED THESE BOATS. LIFE WAS GOOD. WE WEREN'T RICH, BUT WE ALWAYS HAD EVERYTHING WE NEEDED. ALWAYS IN THE BACKGROUND WAS OUR CHURCH. I GREW UP KNOWING THE MASS IN LATIN, SPANISH, AND ENGLISH. I WAS AN ALTAR BOY, AND MY MAMA SANG IN A CHOIR.

I GREW UP KNOWING I WAS DIFFERENT, THOUGH.

Y'SEE. MY MAMA WAS WHITE. POPS WAS "**MESCAN**" THROUGH AND THROUGH.

I REMEMBER FUN PARTIES WITH MY FRIENDS...

...TRAVELING TO TEXAS TO VISIT MY AUNT IN EL PASO.

75

THROUGH IT ALL, THOUGH, THERE WAS SOMETHING AROUND THE EDGES, LURKING.

IT'S THAT MEMORY THAT KEEPS FREAKING ME OUT, NEARLY EVERY NIGHT. IT WON'T GO AWAY.

THEY'RE STANDING THERE. WAITING TO TAKE THEIR REVENGE. WAITING TO GET HIM.

WHEN YOU ENTER A GANG, YOU AIN'T S'POSED TO LEAVE.

AND THE GANG, THEY DON'T FORGET THAT YOU LEFT 'EM.

IT WAS BAD FOR SIX MONTHS, POPS TOLD ME, RIGHT AFTER HE LEFT. I WAS JUST A LITTLE BABY.

BUT THEY QUIT SOON AFTER. HE THOUGHT HE WAS OUT FOR GOOD.

BUT THERE WAS ONE KING, ANTONIO...

HE THOUGHT HE COULD AT LEAST GET SOME CASH OUTTA POPS.

BUT POPS DID ALL HE COULD TO KEEP HIS FAMILY SAFE.

IT WENT ON LIKE THIS FOR YEARS.

AFTER THAT, ALL I WANTED TO DO WAS TO MAKE IT RIGHT FOR POPS.

AND THERE WAS ONLY ONE WAY THAT WAS GONNA HAPPEN.

AND, EVEN THOUGH MY OL' MAN WOULDA GONE LOCO IF HE KNEW IT, I JOINED UP WITH THE *LOGAN HEIGHTS BOYS*.

I WAS GANG BANGIN'. I QUIT SCHOOL. MY MAMA HATED IT. BUT I HAD A REASON... OR SO I THOUGHT.

THE THING IS, I KNEW THOSE BROS MIGHT TURN ON ME ONE DAY TOO, JUST LIKE ANTONIO DID ON MY POPS. I KNEW THAT I COULD ALSO DIE A *CHOLO*, A BANGER. THAT PART SCARED ME. BUT, PART OF ME DIDN'T CARE. I WANTED TO DIE, REALLY. MAYBE THAT'S WHY WHEN I STARTED HITTING METH, I DIDN'T CARE IF IT TOOK OVER ME. I WAS A *MAN ON A MISSION* — ME 'N' THE DEVIL, WE WERE TIGHT. I WANTED *TO KILL ANTONIO* AND *MAKE HIM PAY*.

When I was in school, when pops was still alive, I was a good boy. I did my homework, went to church, respected the law. When I was a *CHOLO* all that was gone. Like I said...

...Me 'n' *SEÑOR DIABLO*, we was tight.

We'd smoke and shoot meth for days. Then we'd drink tequila with meth too. It was a fun time...I thought.

But I got *PARANOID* — more so than my homies, it seemed like. Now, it seems like this is *ALL THAT STICKS WITH ME* — paranoia, *FEAR*.

THAT FEAR WILL LESSEN, MY FRIEND. YOUR BRAIN NEEDS TIME TO HEAL. I DO KNOW A THING OR TWO ABOUT THAT.

WHAT DO YOU KNOW, MAN?

WELL, X IS A LITTLE LIKE METH. I WON'T GET ALL SCIENCY ON YOU, BUT YOU'VE BASICALLY SQUEEZED ALL THE NEUROTRANSMITTERS IN YOUR BRAIN SO HARD, THAT THEY'RE NOT USED TO NOT GETTING HIGH ANYMORE.

I GUESS THAT MAKES SENSE. I GOT TO WHERE I WAS DOING IT ALL THE TIME. AND THEN, I'D SMOKE OR SHOOT AFTER I CAME DOWN, AND THEN THINGS GOT **REALLY NUTS**.

WHAT HAPPENED?

LEMME TELL YA, *CHICA*, IT AIN'T FUN...

CHASING ONE HIT AFTER THE OTHER TO KEEP THE HIGH, I STARTED TO FREAK OUT. I KEPT THINKING THAT ANTONIO WAS OUT TO GET ME AND I HAD TO KILL HIM THAT NIGHT OR HE WAS GONNA GET ME AND MY MOTHER.

FUCK YOU, ANTONIO! *CHINGA TU MADRE!!*

IT GOT TO BE THAT I WAS GETTING HIGH SO MUCH, I WAS STARTIN' TO GO CRAZY, *LOCO*. THE LOGAN HEIGHTS VATOS HAD ENOUGH. I GUESS I GOT OUT THAT WAY.

BY THE TIME I WAS ALMOST EIGHTEEN, I WAS SLEEPING — WHEN I COULD — **WHEREVER** I COULD FIND SPACE.

AFTER I GOT CLEAN AT TREATMENT HERE, SOME DOCTOR TOLD ME THAT I WAS LUCKY. I GUESS I GOT PRETTY MESSED UP AT THAT TIME.

SINCE I WASN'T IN THE GANG NO MORE, I DIDN'T STAND A CHANCE TO KILL ANTONIO, TO GET MY REVENGE. STILL, I HAD TO TRY...

AND THAT'S THE THING...I WAS ONLY A BANGER FOR ABOUT A YEAR. AFTER I GOT OUT, I DID **WHATEVER** I COULD TO SCORE **MERCA** TO PAWN OFF...

...EVEN FROM MY OWN KIN — FROM MY OWN MAMA'S JEWELRY.

I MADE MONEY OTHER WAYS. Y'KNOW... I DID THINGS FOR PEOPLE. THINGS I DON' WANNA REMEMBER. I MULED BAGS FOR **THE REAL BAD GUYS** SOUTH O' THE BORDER — GUYS YOU DON'T **DARE** FUCK WITH. IN IT ALL, I SMOKED IT UP. WHEN I BROKE MY PIPE, I WENT TO THE HOSPITAL BATHROOMS AND BROKE INTO THE NEEDLE CONTAINERS AND SLAMMED MY STASH. I WAS GETTING PRETTY BAD. BUT I HAD A GOAL IN MIND...

YOU WANTED TO FIND **PEACE**. YOU WANTED TO KILL ANTONIO OR BE KILLED BY HIM.

THAT'S RIGHT, BRO. IT WAS MY **LAST FAREWELL RIDE**. I'D BEEN SELLING, SAVING UP FOR MY REVENGE.

MY HOMIES DOWN SOUTH GOT GUNS. **LOTSA GUNS.** I WANTED ANTONIO TO GO OUT GOOD. I WANTED A **CUERNO DE CHIVO**, A "GOAT'S HORN" — THE **AK-47**.

THOSE LAST TWO DAYS, I WAS THINKING A LOT ABOUT HOW I WAS GONNA DO IT. I EVEN STARTED EATIN' BETTER, 'CAUSE I DIDN'T EAT WHEN I WAS SUPER HIGH. I WANTED TO BE **FUERTE**.

SO? WHAT *HAPPENED*? DID YOU GET HIM? WILL YOU *EVEN TELL US*?!

YEAH. I'LL TELL YA.

SO, HERE'S THE THING: I SET UP TO MEET WITH TWO CHOLOS FROM *CÁRTEL DE TIJUANA*.

THEY WAS GONNA SET ME UP WITH MY AK.

SO I MET UP WITH THEM. ONE GUY I RECOGNIZED. THE OTHER I DIDN'T. I GUESS I SHOULD HAVE KNOWN BETTER, 'CAUSE PRETTY SOON I HEARD 'EM. THEN I SAW 'EM...

COPS.

THEY NOT ONLY GOT ME FOR ARMS VIOLATIONS, BUT I HAD THREE EIGHT-BALLS OF CRYSTAL METH ON ME TOO.

85

WHAT THE *FUCK* YOU KNOW ABOUT *HIGHER POWER BS*?!

MY DAD IS *DEAD*. ANTONIO IS STILL *OUT THERE*! WHAT DO I GOT? I TELL YOU WHAT...I GOT *NOTH-ING*. I GOT *NADA*.

I TELL YOU WHAT I GOT TOO. THREE WEEKS HERE. NOBODY GETS WHERE I'M AT. I'M *ALONE*.

WHO ARE *YOU* TO SAY THAT WE'RE ALONE?! I MEAN, EVEN THE *BIG BOOK* TALKS ABOUT THIS IN THE...THE... WHAT CHAPTER WAS IT? OH YEAH, *WE AGNOSTICS*: "WHO ARE *YOU* TO SAY THERE IS *NO GOD*?"

WHATEVER... I'M DONE WITH YOU.

WELL...HE NEEDS MORE RESEARCH, EVIDENTLY.

WHAT DO YOU MEAN, *MORE RESEARCH*?

WHAT I MEAN TO SAY IS THAT SOMETIMES PEOPLE NEED MORE TIME.

PEOPLE NEED TO LEARN THE PROGRAM THEMSELVES. IT CAN'T BE *FORCED* ON THEM. MATT'S MAD AT GOD. I DON'T BLAME HIM. YOU HEARD HIS STORY.

BUT WHY DOESN'T *HE SEE* THAT GOD IS ON HIS SIDE? I MEAN, ACCEPTANCE OF GOD IS *VITAL* TO THE TWELVE STEPS!

COUGH COUGH. AHEM.

LISTEN UP...I DON'T BUY ANY OF THAT GOD TALK. IT'S *HIGHER POWER*, BY THE WAY.

THAT'S RIGHT...I'M GAY *AND AN ATHEIST*! NOT A VERY LIKELY CANDIDATE FOR TWELVE STEP RECOVERY, NO?

BUT THAT'S THE THING WITH THE TWELVE STEPS. THEY AREN'T ABOUT GOD — THEY'RE ABOUT A *HIGHER POWER*. MINE'S THE *RECOVERY GROUP ITSELF*.

BUT...BUT...WHAT ABOUT ALL THE *GOD* LANGUAGE IN THE BIG BOOK? IT'S THERE, Y'KNOW!

HA-HA! THAT'S TRUE, MISS DEBBY! HOWEVER, BILL W. WAS A *BELIEVER* — IT'S ONLY RIGHT THAT HE WROTE LIKE THAT. I'M *NOT*. A BELIEVER, THAT IS...

DIFFERENT PEOPLE RUN A DIFFERENT PROGRAM FOR THEMSELVES. AA IS FLEXIBLE.

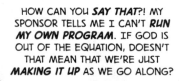

HOW CAN YOU *SAY THAT*?! MY SPONSOR TELLS ME I CAN'T *RUN MY OWN PROGRAM*. IF GOD IS OUT OF THE EQUATION, DOESN'T THAT MEAN THAT WE'RE JUST *MAKING IT UP* AS WE GO ALONG?

I MEAN...OUR CHANCES ARE ALREADY *RAZOR THIN* AS ALCOHOLICS! I'VE SEEN THE NUMBERS ON OUR CHANCES. MY SPONSOR TOLD ME *OVER HALF* THE PEOPLE LEAVE THE PROGRAM IN THEIR FIRST YEAR.

BUT THAT'S THE THING. IT'S A *SIMPLE PROGRAM*. IF WE KEEP GOD IN IT AND WORK IT, IT *DOES* WORK!

THE WAY I FIGURE IT ALL, GOD HAS TO BE PART OF THE PROGRAM. HOW CAN IT BE ANY OTHER WAY? IT'S **SIMPLE**. FIRST, WE NEED TO LOOK AT OURSELVES...

STEP FOUR
"Made a searching and fearless moral inventory of ourselves."

AND — BELIEVE ME — I KNOW WHAT THAT'S LIKE. STEP FOUR IS EASY. ACTUALLY **DOING IT** ISN'T. LOOKING AT THE MESS I MADE WITH MY LIFE WAS NO FUN.

BUT I GOT TO A PLACE WHERE I COULDN'T GO ANYWHERE ELSE. SO, I TURNED TO GOD.

IN 2004, I LIVED WITH MY BOYFRIEND, MARK, IN LEHIGH ACRES, FLORIDA. THE PLACE **WAS** BOOMING. BUT THAT ALL CHANGED IN 2007. THE HOUSING BUBBLE POPPED WITH A **BANG**.

MARK WORKED IN CONSTRUCTION. SO HE PRETTY MUCH LOST HIS JOB AFTER THE COLLAPSE. THEN HE GOT ABUSIVE. HE *USED* ME. I WASN'T GOING DOWN THAT PATH AGAIN. WHEN I WAS LITTLE...

...I WAS NOT ONLY ABUSED *PHYSICALLY* BY MY DAD...MY BROTHER *MOLESTED ME*!

SO, I WASN'T GOING TO TAKE IT ANYMORE. IT WAS 2009.

AFTER MARK WAS GONE, I DIDN'T HAVE A WAY TO PAY FOR THINGS. I TRIED...

...AND I TRIED...

...AND *TRIED AGAIN*.

BUT LET'S FACE IT. WHEN YOU ONLY HAVE A HIGH SCHOOL DIPLOMA AND YOUR BOYFRIEND'S BEEN THE *ONLY ONE* WHO'S EVER PROVIDED FOR YOU...

...YOU TAKE ANYTHING YOU CAN GET.

AND, YOU SEE, I ALREADY CALLED THE CALL CENTER TO TALK TO A MANAGER, AND THEY SAID THAT I HAD TO SPEAK WITH YOU ABOUT THE REFUND. I DON'T HAVE TIME FOR THIS, BECAUSE I NEED TO...

UH-HUH. YES. I UNDERSTAND. YES, MA'AM.

WORK AT THE CALL CENTER SUCKED. BUT I TOOK IT. I NEEDED MONEY.

MY PARENTS SAID THAT THEY COULD HELP ME WITH THE MONEY I NEEDED. I GUESS IT WAS BECAUSE THEY WANTED MY BOYS TO BE HAPPY. THING IS...

...I WASN'T HAPPY. NOT AT ALL.

I TRIED DATING. BUT WHEN YOU HAVE TO WORK 50, 60 HOURS A WEEK AND YOU HAVE TWO KIDS TO LOOK AFTER, THAT DOESN'T PAN OUT TOO WELL. MY MOM AND DAD DIDN'T HELP THE SITUATION. MY MOM KEPT ASKING ABOUT MY PLANS. "WHAT PLANS?" I THOUGHT. I WAS JUST TRYING TO MAKE ENDS MEET — KEEP MY HEAD ABOVE WATER.

SO I DEALT WITH IT...

I DID THIS, DAY IN, DAY OUT, FOR TWO-AND-A-HALF YEARS.

THAT'S WHAT I DID EVERY NIGHT. I THOUGHT I WAS NORMAL. ISN'T THAT WHAT PEOPLE DO? WELL, THEN I CAME HERE...TO GET BETTER.

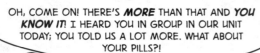

OH, COME ON! THERE'S **MORE** THAN THAT AND **YOU KNOW IT**! I HEARD YOU IN GROUP IN OUR UNIT TODAY; YOU TOLD US A LOT MORE. WHAT ABOUT YOUR PILLS?!

YOU...**YOU**...HOW COULD **YOU** SAY **THAT**?! YOU LITTLE **PRISSY**... P—PR—**PRINCESS!** THAT WAS **PRIVATE** IN OUR GROUP! DON'T YOU KNOW IT'S **AGAINST** THE PROGRAM TO DO THAT?! **BESIDES THAT, YOU—**

LET'S JUST **CALM DOWN**. IT'S EASY TO GET WORKED UP WHEN YOU FEEL LIKE YOU'RE TRAPPED. THAT'S PART OF THE PROCESS — IT'S LIKE WE GO BACK TO OUR ANIMAL NATURE. IT'S A **FIGHT-OR-FLIGHT** THING. THERE'S A REASON WE HAVE THE PHRASE "**EASY DOES IT**" IN AA.

BUT...I GOTTA SAY. T'WASN'T VERY NICE OF YA, HANNAH-GIRL. YOU KNOW HOW IT GOES..."**WHAT YOU SAY HERE, WHAT YOU HEAR HERE, STAYS HERE.**"

NICE JOB, HANNAH. YOU CAN'T DO **ANYTHING** RIGHT!

WHAT'S SAID IS SAID. **IS THERE** MORE TO YOUR STORY, DEBBY? YOU KNOW WE ONLY WANT TO **LISTEN**...IN THIS PROGRAM, WE LOVE YOU UNTIL **YOU WANT TO LOVE YOURSELF.** IT'S WHAT IT'S ABOUT. WE'VE ALL BEEN THERE.

NO, THERE *IS* MORE. HANNAH'S RIGHT. IT'S JUS— IT'S JUST THAT I CAN'T BE-LIEVE IT MYSELF...THAT I GOT *THAT BAD*.

FACT IS, AFTER MARK LEFT I WAS SAD. REALLY, *REALLY SAD*. CLINICALLY DEPRESSED, IN FACT. AND TRYING TO TURN TO GOD *DIDN'T SEEM TO HELP*. I PRAYED, SO HARD. I JUST WANTED TO FEEL *NORMAL* AGAIN... WHATEVER THAT WAS. I WENT TO DOCTORS FOR HELP, BUT...

...ONE TIME DIDN'T SEEM TO BE ENOUGH. I WENT TO OTHER DOCTORS, AND...UM...I LIED.

I LIED TO GET MORE PILLS. XANAX.

AND ANTIDEPRESSANTS. HATED THOSE...

AND MORE XANAX. VALIUM. LORAZEPAM. *BENZOS...*

I LIED AND I LIED AND I LIED AGAIN. THING IS, I KNEW I WAS LYING, BUT I COULDN'T DO ANY-THING ELSE. I NEEDED WHAT I NEEDED. I NEED TO QUIT LYING. IT'S MY GOAL; I JUST CAN'T...SEEM TO REACH IT.

S'ALRIGHT. JUNKIES LIE. IT'S *WHAT WE DO*. YOU'RE NOT LYING NOW, THOUGH.

THAT'S THE REASON, ALEX, WHY I THINK I NEED GOD. GOD KEEPS ME STRAIGHT *WITH MYSELF*.

THAT'S FINE. *FOR YOU.* DON'T STUFF IT DOWN MY GULLET...I GOT MY OWN ISSUES TO DEAL WITH. HE-HE.

WHY CAN'T I COME UP WITH AN ANSWER *FOR ME*?

YOU JUST GOTTA UNDERSTAND...EVERYTHING... *EVERYTHING* STARTED TO WEIGH ME DOWN!

MORTGAGE BILL
PAST DUE

I COULDN'T MAKE MY PAYMENTS FOR MY HOUSE. WHEN MARK AND I HOOKED UP, I HAD SOME MONEY FROM MY GRANDPARENTS I USED FOR A DOWN PAYMENT FOR THE HOUSE. IT WAS IN MY NAME. MARK PAID THE MORTGAGE WHEN HE WAS WITH ME. WHEN HE LEFT, I TOOK IT OVER. BUT IT WASN'T LONG BEFORE THE HOUSE WAS UNDERWATER. TO MAKE MATTERS WORSE, MY PARENTS JUST KEPT TELLING ME TO STRAIGHTEN MYSELF OUT. THEY COULD SEE I WAS A MESS. I HATED MY JOB. I WANTED TO FORGET ALL OF IT WHEN I GOT HOME. AND...MY BOYS...*OH GOD!*

I CAN'T BELIEVE I LOST MY BOYS! I...I... *CAN'T GO ON!*

TELL US WHAT HAPPENED...

GET IT OUT. THE PAIN DOESN'T HAVE AS MUCH POWER WHEN YOU SHARE IT.

I GUESS IT ALL STARTED WITH MY DEPRESSION. AND WITH ME TRYING TO HANDLE IT MYSELF. THAT'S WHY I FIRST WENT TO THE DOCTORS, TO GET BETTER. ALL THEY DID — ALL *I DID* — WAS MAKE IT WORSE. DRINKING WITH MY MEDS MADE ME BLACK OUT. IT WAS SCARY...BUT IT WAS COMFORTING TOO. THAT MAKE SENSE?

TOTALLY.

I STARTED LOSING THINGS. FIRST, IT WAS MY STUFF.

THEN I LOST MY JOB.

WE CAN'T HAVE YOU ZONING OUT, MS. DAVIES. I'M SORRY, BUT WE NEED TO LET YOU GO.

I MOVED IN WITH A GIRLFRIEND, JUANITA. BUT ALL I DID WAS SLEEP. AND DRINK. AND DRUG.

I HONESTLY DON'T REMEMBER ALL THAT MUCH. TAKING MY MEDS AND DRINKING ON TOP OF THEM PUT EVERYTHING IN A BLUR...A HAZE.

IT'S LIKE IT'S ALL GRAY... LIKE A MOVIE ON A SCREEN TOO FAR AWAY.

BUT I REMEMBER WHAT MATTERS...

95

NEXT THING I KNEW, I WAS IN A ROOM BY MYSELF. I HAD BANDAGES ON MY WRISTS. I DIDN'T KNOW HOW THEY HAD GOTTEN THERE. **WHAT DID I DO? WHERE ARE MY BOYS? ARE THEY SAFE?** I HAD SO MANY QUESTIONS.

BUT THE BIGGEST QUESTION I HAD — EVEN MORE THAN WHERE I WAS, WHAT HAD HAPPENED, OR WHETHER MY BOYS WERE SAFE — WAS THE ONE THING I KNEW I COULDN'T LIVE WITHOUT:

WHERE ARE MY PILLS?!

SINCE I'VE COME HERE, THEY TELL ME THAT BENZOS — ESPECIALLY WHEN YOU DRINK TOO — ARE LIKE THAT. THEY MAKE YOU **BLACK OUT.** AND THE DOSAGE I WAS TAKING COULD HAVE **KILLED** ME, COMING OFF THEM. BUT I THANK GOD FOR THE PEOPLE WHO WERE THERE FOR ME.

96

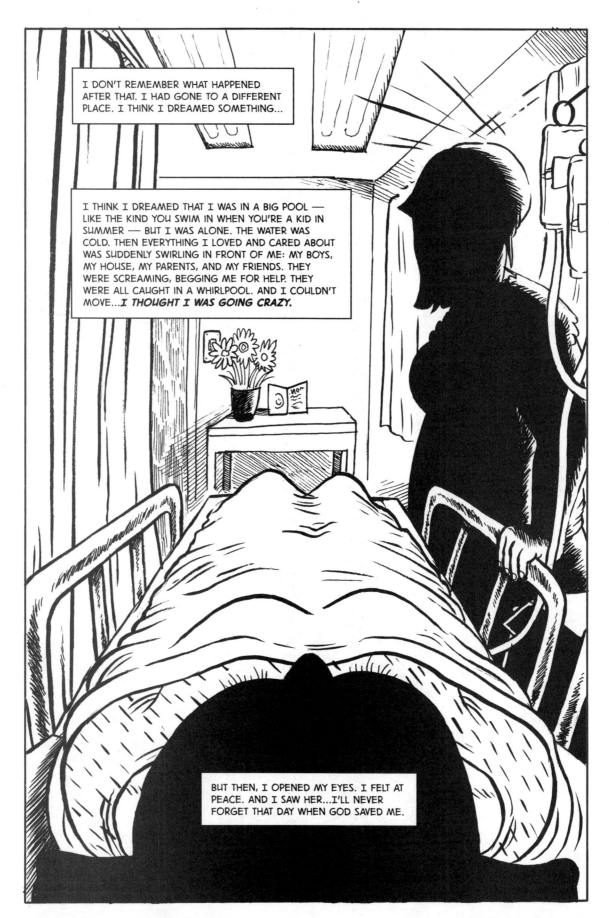

IT WAS GRETCHEN. I HAD KNOWN HER SINCE HIGH SCHOOL. WE WERE FRIENDS, AND, NOT LONG AFTER, WE DRIFTED APART.

YOU SEE, ALEX...THERE **IS** A GOD. AND HE SENT HIS GUARDIAN ANGEL TO ME.

WHAT ARE YOU DOING HERE?

YOUR PARENTS CALLED ME. THEY TOLD ME WHAT HAPPENED TO YOU. I'M **LIKE YOU**, DEBBY. I'M AN **ALCOHOLIC**. BUT I'VE FOUND **RECOVERY**. YOU CAN TOO!

IT SURPRISED ME...NO, IT **SHOCKED** ME. SHE AND I HAD BEEN PRETTY GOOD FRIENDS IN HIGH SCHOOL IN FORT MYERS. BUT I NEVER KNEW SHE HAD A **PROBLEM**. I MEAN, WE PARTIED, LIKE **ANYONE** DOES GROWING UP. BUT SHE TOLD ME THAT SHE SPIRALED OUT OF CONTROL SOON AFTER. I HADN'T KNOWN.

GRETCHEN WAS THE ONE WHO GOT ME SOBER. WELL, HER, AND **GOD TOO**. ANYWAY...YOU KNOW HOW IT GOES. I CAME TO TREATMENT HERE. SHE'S BEEN REALLY SUPPORTIVE OF ME TOO. I'VE GOT TWO WEEKS LEFT, AND I'M DOING MY **FIFTH STEP** WITH HER. I'M SO EXCITED TO FINALLY BE SOBER AND EVERYTHING.

WELL...HOLD ON. I DON'T MEAN TO QUESTION YOU AGAIN, BUT...COME ON. WHAT HAPPENED TO YOU? DO YOU KNOW?

AND...UM, I'M REALLY SORRY FOR BEING A BITCH AND ALL BEFORE. IT'S JUST THAT, I REALLY WANNA KNOW. Y'KNOW WHAT I MEAN?

WELL, LET ME TELL YOU. IT WASN'T GOOD. I ALMOST CAN'T EVEN **BEAR** TO THINK ABOUT MY BOYS. BUT...IT HAS TO WORK OUT, RIGHT? I MEAN, I'M **SOBER** NOW!

I GUESS I HAD GONE COMPLETELY *BATSHIT CRAZY* WHEN I WAS ON MY BENZOS. I THREATENED TO KILL MY PARENTS IF THEY TOOK MY BOYS. THEY CALLED THE COPS AND HAD ME COMMITTED. THEN, IN THE PSYCH WARD, I TRIED TO PUNCTURE MY WRISTS WITH A BALLPOINT PEN. I DON'T REMEMBER *ANY OF THIS*.

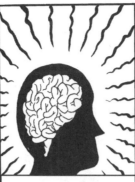

THEN I HAD A *WITHDRAWAL SEIZURE*. THEY TOLD ME IT IS BASICALLY LIKE YOUR BRAIN PLUGS INTO A *WALL SOCKET*. ALL THE LITTLE BRAIN CELLS FIRE *ALL AT ONCE*.

THEN THEY TOLD ME — SORRY...THIS PART IS REALLY HARD. THEY TOLD ME IF I DIDN'T GET CLEAN, THAT I'D LOSE MY BOYS. MY PARENTS — MY OWN PARENTS — ARE GOING TO TAKE THEM AWAY FROM ME!

BUT...I GOTTA HAVE HOPE. I'M LOOKING FORWARD TO *CLEANING MY SIDE OF THE STREET*. I'M READY FOR *STEP FIVE*.

STEP FIVE

*"Admitted to God,
to ourselves, and
to another human being
the exact nature
of our wrongs."*

I FIGURE, I'VE ALREADY HAD A *SPIRITUAL EXPERIENCE* WITH GRETCHEN IN THE HOSPITAL. GOD MET ME. NOW, I NEED TO MEET HIM. THEN I CAN GET MY KIDS BACK!

BUT...LISTEN NOW. IT'S NOT LIKE THAT, YOU'VE GOT T—

AHEM.

SHH. IT'S OKAY...

Bedford Hills, New York—
Present Day

...AND THE ONLY WAY I GOT SOBER WAS TO GET MY ASS TO MEETINGS. IT'S FUNNY ALL THOSE YEARS HOW I MADE EXCUSES—

OH! HEY...

GLAD YOU COULD MAKE IT! WE'RE AT *BILL W.'S HOME*, THE PLACE WHERE HE LIVED IN THE LAST YEARS BEFORE HE DIED. BILL W., YOU RECALL, IS THE COFOUNDER OF *ALCOHOLICS ANONYMOUS* AND THE ONE WHO GAVE US THE *TWELVE STEPS* AS WE KNOW THEM TODAY.

SPENCER AND I WANTED YOU TO SEE THIS PLACE, BECAUSE WE WANTED TO SHOW YOU SOMETHING...

COME ON. FOLLOW US. THIS IS PRETTY COOL...

THIS IS *BILL W.'S* OFFICE. HE WROTE A LETTER HERE ONE COLD JANUARY DAY IN *1961*.

BILL WROTE A LETTER TO A GUY NAMED *CARL JUNG*. HE WAS A FAMOUS PSYCHIATRIST FROM SWITZERLAND.

CARL GUSTAV JUNG — *PRONOUNCED YOONG* — HAD A CONNECTION WITH BILL W. THROUGH AN AMAZING COINCIDENCE. DR. JUNG HAD TREATED A MAN, ROWLAND H., WHO KNEW A MAN NAMED EBBY T., WHO KNEW BILL W. AND HELPED HIM GET SOBER, WHICH LED TO BILL TRACKING DOWN DR. BOB AND FOUNDING *AA*. AND ALL THIS IN A *TIME BEFORE FACEBOOK*!

IN THE LETTER, BILL THANKED DR. JUNG, RECALLING THE STORY BILL HAD HEARD FROM ROWLAND, THE MAN WHO HAD SEEN THE GOOD DOCTOR. HE HAD VISITED DR. JUNG AS A LAST-DITCH EFFORT, AND DR. JUNG TOLD ROWLAND THAT HIS CASE WAS PRETTY MUCH *HOPELESS*.

WHEN I GOT SOBER, THAT WASN'T THE WAY IT WAS *AT ALL*. MY *TWELVE STEP RECOVERY* WAS MORE A *GRADUAL, PERSISTENT* TRANSFORMATION. A LOT OF PEOPLE — IN FACT, MOST — HAVE SIMILAR EXPERIENCES THAT COME AS A RESULT OF WORKING THE STEPS. AND THAT'S *OKAY!*

PEOPLE WHO WORK THE TWELVE STEPS THOROUGHLY, IN THE ORDER THEY WERE WRITTEN, CAN HAVE ALL KINDS OF SPIRITUAL AWAKENINGS — OR "CONVERSIONS" AS DR. JUNG CALLED THEM — BUT IT'S THEIR *OWN CONVERSION* WITH THEIR *OWN PERSONAL HIGHER POWER.*

BY THE WAY...THAT'S WHY LARRY TOOK THE LEAD TO ALLOW DEBBY TO HAVE *HER OWN EXPERIENCE*. HER RECOVERY HAS TO BE *HER OWN*, NO MATTER HOW MUCH WE'D LIKE TO TELL HER WHAT TO DO OR WHAT TO THINK.

COME ON...FOLLOW US. SPENCER'S GOT SOMETHING ELSE HE WANTS TO SHOW US.

POP!

WHOA!

AH! NICE! THERE'S NOTHING LIKE THE *SWISS AIR* — IT'S THE *ALPS*. SO *CLEAN*...

NICE THAT YOU BROUGHT US HERE, SPENCER...WE MUST BE GOING TO THE *C.G. JUNG INSTITUTE*!

BY THE WAY...IF YA GOTTA GO TO SWITZERLAND, THIS IS A GREAT WAY TO TRAVEL. BEATS FLYING ANY DAY!

RM104

HERE IT IS. THERE IS A LOT. PLEASE LEAVE ANYTHING YOU FIND ON THE TABLE. I WILL REPLACE IT AFTER YOU FINISH.

Danke schön.

COME ON, SPENCE. LET'S GET AT IT.

MAN, WHERE IS IT? THIS IS LIKE SEARCHING FOR A NEEDLE IN A HAYSTACK!

WAIT...HERE. HERE IT IS!

"THE ONLY RIGHT AND LEGITIMATE WAY TO SUCH AN EXPERIENCE [OF RECOVERY] IS...WHEN YOU WALK ON A PATH, WHICH LEADS YOU TO HIGHER UNDERSTANDING."

"YOU SEE, ALCOHOL IN LATIN IS 'SPIRITUS' AND YOU USE THE SAME WORD FOR THE HIGHEST RELIGIOUS EXPERIENCE AS WELL AS FOR THE MOST DEPRAVING POISON. THE HELPFUL FORMULA THEREFORE IS: 'SPIRITUS CONTRA SPIRITUM.'"

AH...*I GET IT!* I'VE HEARD THIS BEFORE, WHEN I WAS IN TREATMENT. IT MEANS: *SPIRITUALITY AGAINST ALCOHOL*. THE SIGNIFICANCE IS THAT WE FIND OUT HOW TO LIVE LIFE WITHOUT CHEMICALS AND *REALLY LIVE IT* BY CONNECTING WITH *OTHERS WHO HAVE THE SAME PROBLEM* AND OUR *HIGHER POWER*.

AND, AFTER WE CLEAN HOUSE WITH *STEPS FOUR* AND *FIVE*, WE THEN DEDICATE OURSELVES TO THE PROGRAM. THESE STEPS MAKE US LOOK AT OUR *DEFECTS OF CHARACTER* THAT DRIVE US TO *ADDICTIVE THINKING* AND CAUSE US TO ADOPT A *LIFESTYLE* THAT *REINFORCES OUR DRINKING AND DRUGGING*!

DR. CARL JUNG AND *BILL W.* KNEW THAT, FOR AN ALCOHOLIC TO TURN HIS OR HER LIFE IN THE RIGHT DIRECTION, THERE HAD TO BE A COMMITMENT, A *SURRENDER*, TO THAT NEW WAY OF LIFE.

AND THAT, MY FRIENDS, IS ALL THAT *STEPS SIX* AND *SEVEN* ARE ABOUT — A *COMMITMENT* TO SURRENDER EVERYTHING FROM OUR PAST THAT WILL KEEP US FROM *CLIMBING TO THE PEAK*!

STEP SIX
"Were entirely ready to have God remove all these defects of character."

STEP SEVEN
"Humbly asked Him to remove our shortcomings."

YEAH. THAT'S THE THING ABOUT ADDICTION, DEBBY — IT LEAVES WRECKAGE NOT ONLY IN OUR PAST, BUT BY OUR *CONTINUING BEHAVIORS* WE HAVE AS ADDICTS AND ALCOHOLICS.

I DON'T WANT TO MAKE YOU FEEL BAD OR SHAME YOU IN ANY WAY — LORD KNOWS YOU'VE HAD ENOUGH OF THAT — IT'S THAT WE NEED TO HEAR THE GENTLE VOICE OF THE PROGRAM IF WE'RE TO *GAIN PERSPECTIVE* ABOUT OURSELVES.

BELIEVE IT OR NOT, THIS STUFF IS STILL TOUGH FOR ME. I TALK TO MY SPONSOR REGULARLY, BECAUSE I NEED HIM TO *CHECK MY ACTIONS*. OUR ACCOUNTABILITY WORKS THROUGH SURRENDERING OUR WILL AND SEEKING THE GUIDANCE OF SOMEONE WHO'S ALREADY WALKED *THE SAME PATH WE'RE WALKING*.

MAKING AMENDS ISN'T JUST FOR THE STUFF WE DID WHILE WE WERE DEEP IN OUR ADDICTIONS. IT'S ALSO ABOUT A *CONTINUING LIFESTYLE* WHERE WE CHALLENGE OURSELVES DAILY.

MAKING AMENDS ISN'T JUST SAYING *WE'RE SORRY*, EITHER. IT'S A REAL, GENUINE *ATTITUDE-WITH-ACTION* TO MAKE THINGS RIGHT.

107

OF COURSE, WE HAVE
TO ATTEMPT TO CLEAN
UP THE WRECKAGE
FROM THE PAST, FIRST.

STEP EIGHT
*"Made a list of all persons
we had harmed,
and became willing
to make amends to them all."*

I REMEMBER DOING
MY STEP EIGHT. IT
WASN'T EASY. IN FACT,
IT WAS ***TERRIFYING***...

...TERRIFYING,
NOT IN WRITING
THE LIST ITSELF.

IT CAN BE SCARY, BECAUSE WE KNOW THAT STEP
NINE ASKS US TO ***FOLLOW THROUGH*** WITH OUR
WILLINGNESS TO ACTUALLY ***MAKE*** THOSE AMENDS. IT
HELPED ME WHEN MY SPONSOR REMINDED ME THAT
STEP EIGHT IS JUST ABOUT MAKING THE LIST, AND I
COULD DEAL WITH MAKING EACH AMEND WHEN THE
TIME CAME.

SOME OF THESE ENCOUNTERS GO WELL.

UH...I DON'T KNOW HOW
TO SAY THIS. YOU WERE THE AR-
RESTING OFFICERS, AND YOU SAVED
MY LIFE WHEN I CRASHED INTO
THE STATE CAPITOL BUILDING. I
WANT TO MAKE THINGS RIGHT AND
COME CLEAN ABOUT THE WAY I
BEHAVED THAT DAY.

I WAS TOTALLY
OUT OF LINE,
AND I —

I KNOW WHERE YOU'RE AT, MY
FRIEND. I'M A ***FRIEND OF BILL***. AND,
WE WERE JUST DOING OUR JOB.

WE CAN'T CONTROL HOW PEOPLE REACT WHEN WE TRY TO MAKE AMENDS. RELINQUISHING CONTROL — *LETTING GO* — IS HARD FOR US. IT'S HARD, BUT *ABSOLUTELY NECESSARY*!

STEP NINE
"Made direct amends to such people wherever possible, except when to do so would injure them or others."

WHAT'S *THAT* SUPPOSED TO MEAN?

WHAT'S THAT? YOU MEAN THE WHOLE PART ABOUT *INJURING OTHERS*?

YEAH.

WELL, THAT'S STRAIGHTFORWARD, HANNAH-GIRL. SOMETIMES THE SHIT WE DO IN ADDICTION WE NEED TO KEEP TO OURSELVES, OR WE'LL END UP DOING *MORE DAMAGE*.

WELL...COULDN'T WE JUST LET ALL OUR AMENDS SLIDE BECAUSE WE THINK "THEY MIGHT HURT OTHERS"?

HA! YES, MA'AM! YOU *CAN* DO THAT. BUT, THEN, YOU WON'T BE *WORKING THIS STEP*!

I'LL TELL YA SOMETHIN'...THERE WAS A CHAP I KNEW IN NA IN SOUTH LONDON. HE DIDN'T DOSE A FRIEND O' HIS RIGHT, AND HIS FRIEND ENDED UP *SNUFFIN' IT* — ER...*HE DIED*. HE COULDN'T GO BACK AND *UN-KILL* HIS FRIEND. BUT, WHEN HE GOT SOBER HE SHARED HIS *EXPERIENCE, STRENGTH, AND HOPE*. PLUS, HE FILLED OUT AN ORGAN-DONOR CARD. SO, THERE'S ALWAYS *SOMETHIN'* Y'CAN DO.

MATT. UH...I WANTED TO...UM... SAY SOMETHING.

YEAH. WHAT'S THAT?

UM...I DUNNO. I JUST WANTED TO SAY I'M SORRY THA—

THE THING 'BOUT YOU IS YOU FUCKIN' THINK YOU KNOW EVERYTHING!

YOU HAVE **NO CLUE** HOW HARD IT'S BEEN FOR ME!

MY DAD, HE WAS **KILLED**! AND THERE AIN'T NOTHING TO DO 'BOUT IT. GETTING HIGH — IT **WORKS**. NOW I CAN'T DO THAT! WHAT I S'POSED TO DO?!

WHAT I S'POSED TO DO?!

¡NO PUEDO AGUANTAR ESTO!

I GET IT... I DO.

I'VE BEEN TO THAT SAME **WALL**, MATT; I DIDN'T KNOW WHERE TO GO. I DIDN'T THINK I COULD TAKE IT ANYMORE, EITHER. WHAT I'M TRYING TO SAY IS...I DUNNO. I GUESS I REALLY WANT TO MAKE THINGS RIGHT BETWEEN US. I'M THE ONE WHO MAKES ASSUMP-TIONS. I WANT EVERYTHING TO BE **BLACK-AND-WHITE**, BECAUSE I'M REALLY **AFRAID**.

I AM SORRY. WHAT CAN I DO TO HELP?

113

OKAY, OKAY. HOW 'BOUT WE JOIN THE OTHERS?
...TO GIVE EACH OTHER A CHANCE TO KNOW WHAT GETTING SOBER IS ABOUT.
BUT, THAT'S HARD!
HA! NO ONE SAID THIS IS EASY, HANNAH-GIRL. IT'S EASY TO UNDER-STAND, BUT DOING IT IS ANOTHER THING!
OH...MATT! GOOD TO SEE YOU! YOU AND DEBBY GET A CHANCE TO TALK?
YEAH. WE TALKED.
OKAY. LET'S SEE WHAT YOU THINK ABOUT WHAT WE WERE TALKING ABOUT...
I WAS ASKING WHY WE NEED TO KEEP GOING TO MEETINGS. WHY IS IT THAT WE CAN'T GET SOBER, AND GET ON WITH OUR LIVES? WHY ALL THIS CONTINUED STEP WORK? WHY KEEP DWELLING AND OBSESSING ON OUR PROBLEMS WHEN WE SHOULD JUST GET ON?!
OH YEAH. THAT. YOU'RE TALKING ABOUT STEP TEN WORK.
STEP TEN "Continued to take personal inventory and when we were wrong promptly admitted it."

WELL, JUST 'CAUSE I'M THE YOUNGEST ONE HERE AT *EIGHTEEN* DOESN'T MEAN I'M AN IDIOT! I KNOW *STEP TEN!*

IT'S NOT LIKE NO ONE'S TOLD ME THIS EVERY. *SINGLE.* **DAY!**

IT'S JUST THAT, WHY CAN'T PEOPLE, LIKE, SEE THAT THIS RECOVERY STUFF DOESN'T HAVE TO BE SO HARD?

AND...THERE'S THIS COMPLETE LACK OF CONFIDENCE IN *MY ABILITY TO LEARN* HOW TO QUIT. I MEAN, I GET IT. LET'S FIX IT AND *MOVE ON!*

AND I'LL TELL YOU SOMETHING ELSE: I'VE BEEN *AN OPEN BOOK* — COMPLETELY HONEST — ABOUT WHAT I'VE DONE. I SAY WHY *REHASH* THE PAST?

HEY NOW...LET'S RESPECT HER.

WHAT?! WHAT'S SO *GODDAMN* FUNNY?!!

WHY ISN'T MY POINT OF VIEW *VALID*?! I HAVE *MY OWN STORY* TOO!

IF YOU WANNA HEAR ME OUT...

...MAYBE YOU'LL LEARN SOMETHING.

TRAVIS — THAT WAS HIS NAME — WAS LIKE THE CENTER OF A BIKE'S WHEEL. EVERY SPOKE WENT RIGHT TO THE CENTER, WHERE HE WAS. HE LIKED TO DRINK AND PARTY. PRETTY SOON, I DID TOO. BUT I GOT EVEN FATTER AND HE DIDN'T LIKE IT. I FOUND A **SOLUTION** FOR THAT, THOUGH...

BLARG!

I GOT TO BE PRETTY GOOD AT IT TOO.

NOBODY KNEW. WELL... BACK THEN, ANYWAY. I WAS QUIET AND SNEAKY AT IT.

SKULL KICK!

ALL I KNEW IS THAT TRAVIS RESPONDED TO MY NEW BODY. AND I LOVED HIM.

MAYBE THAT'S THE REASON WHY I LOVED HIM SO MUCH. HE TOOK ME AWAY FROM **PODUNKVILLE** TO A NEW AND EXCITING PLACE.

OF COURSE...AND I KNOW THIS NOW...EVERY ACTION HAS A CONSEQUENCE.

pregnant

not pregnant

MY PARENTS WERE OBLIVIOUS TO ALL THIS. THEY WORSHIPPED THE GROUND I WALKED ON.

THEY DIDN'T HAVE A CLUE.

YEAH. I SURE DUPED THEM. WELL...BACK THEN. BUT WITH ALL THAT HAPPENED, TRAVIS DEVISED A PLAN. WE SAID THAT WE WANTED A "ROMANTIC GETAWAY" TO CHICAGO OVERNIGHT. TRAVIS HAD RELATIVES THERE, SO THEY'D, LIKE, CHAPERONE. AMAZINGLY, MY PARENTS LET ME GO. I'D JUST TURNED SEVENTEEN.

Planned Parenthood

OPEN

AND, WELL...I DID WHAT I THOUGHT I NEEDED TO DO.

WISCO... 22 Mi...

AND THAT WAS THAT.

EXCEPT TRAVIS HAD TO GET SOME *CANDY* FROM THE CITY FOR US TO TAKE BACK HOME.

IT WAS A WHOLE *SHITLOAD* OF PILLS.

AND IT WAS *ALL OURS*.

THE REST OF THAT SUMMER, WE PARTIED...

...AND WE PARTIED. DRINKING AND EATIN' THOSE PILLS.

tickle tickle

GHS

AND, LIKE A FAIRYTALE, I THOUGHT THAT LIFE WAS GOOD.

BUT ALL THINGS FINALLY COME TO AN END...

SOME MANAGE TO EVEN COME TO A GOOD END, DESPITE OURSELVES.

I MANAGED TO STILL GRADUATE AT THE TOP OF MY CLASS.

THOUGH, WHEN I THINK ABOUT IT, MY GRADES WERE ONLY WHAT THEY WERE, BECAUSE I WAS ALREADY SO AHEAD OF EVERYONE ELSE.

ONE EVENING IN THE SUMMER AFTER HIGH SCHOOL GRADUATION, I WENT TO SURPRISE TRAVIS AT HIS HOME.

BUT, IT DIDN'T LOOK LIKE HE WAS HOME.

TRAVIS?

OF COURSE, I THOUGHT TO MYSELF THAT TRAVIS HAD GONE OUT WITH HIS BUDDIES.

IF THERE IS ONE CONNECTION I CAN MAKE WITH THE TWELVE STEPS, IT'S THAT I THINK THEY SHOW US THAT MUCH OF LIFE IS *BEYOND OUR CONTROL*.

TRAAA-VIS... ARE YOU HOME?

LIFE'S BEYOND OUR CONTROL...AND SO ARE *OTHER PEOPLE*!

TRAVIS... HUMPH. **ASSHOLE!**

I KNOW, RIGHT?

THING IS... THAT SET ME OFF.

WHEN YOU THINK YOUR WORLD IS FALLING APART, YOU DO EVERYTHING YOU KNOW TO PUT IT BACK TOGETHER THE WAY **YOU** WANT.

AS AN ALCOHOLIC AND ADDICT, THE WAY I PUT IT "BACK TOGETHER" IS TO RUN TO WHAT I KNOW. FOR ME, THAT'S DRUGS AND ALCOHOL.

I'M WHAT YOU'D CALL A **HIGH ACHIEVER**. WHEN I WANT SOMETHING, I GO ALL OUT. SO, SUMMER BEFORE COLLEGE, I HIT IT **HARD**.

THAT'S FAIRLY COMMON. **MANY** ADDICTS AND ALCOHOLICS ARE HIGH ACHIEVERS. IF YOU MANAGE TO STAY SOBER, THAT CAN BE A GREAT ASSET FOR YOU, HANNAH.

NO DOUBT...

MY LIFE MOVED ON. AS I PACKED TO GO TO COLLEGE IN A NEARBY STATE, MY ONLY THOUGHTS WERE HOW **FUN** COLLEGE WAS GOING TO BE. I COULDN'T WAIT TO PARTY. STILL, I KEPT EVERYTHING HIDDEN FROM MY FAMILY...

IN A WAY, I THINK MY USAGE WAS, LIKE, EVEN HIDDEN FROM **MYSELF**. I HAD NO CLUE HOW **OUT OF CONTROL** I WAS.

EVERY DAY, *JUST WAKING UP* GOT TO BE HARD. I MISSED CLASSES. I STOPPED TALKING WITH MY PARENTS. AND...*SOMETHING ELSE*...

BEEP!

BEEP!

BEEP!

BEEP!

...I FORGOT TO MENTION IT: THAT SUMMER I CAUGHT TRAVIS CHEATING, I STARTED *BINGE EATING*. I WAS GETTING FAT AGAIN.

SO MANY OF MY FRIENDS TOOK MEDS FOR THEIR *ADHD*, AND I DISCOVERED IF I TOOK THEM, I WASN'T AS HUNGRY. AND, I WAS *HIGH*.

I TRIED TO GET THEM WHEREVER AND WHENEVER I COULD. OR OTHER PILLS TOO — VIKES, XANAX, PERCS, *WHATEVER*.

THING IS...THOSE THINGS ARE *DAMN EXPENSIVE*! AND I WASN'T EXACTLY SWIMMING IN CASH.

FOR ADDICTS, THIS IS JUST ANOTHER OPPORTUNITY FOR US TO USE *OUR CREATIVITY* TO FIND PILLS WHERE WE CAN. EVEN IN OUR PARENTS' FRIENDS' *MEDICINE CABINETS*!!

IT GETS TO THE POINT WHERE YOU'RE WILLING TO GO *TO ANY LENGTH* TO GET TO A PLACE WHERE THERE ISN'T THE PAIN. IT'S NOT ABOUT GETTING HIGH ANYMORE — IT'S ABOUT JUST *STOPPING THE PAIN*.

AND THEN, WE GO TO OTHER PAINFUL PLACES...

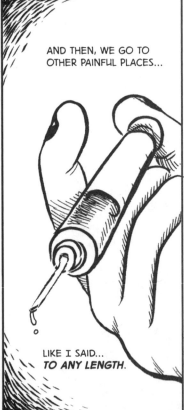

LIKE I SAID... *TO ANY LENGTH*.

AND I OD'D. THANK GOD THE STATE I WAS LIVING IN HAD A "GOOD SAMARITAN" LAW AND A MORE ENLIGHTENED UNDERSTANDING OF ADDICTION. SOMEONE THERE GAVE ME **NALOXONE** — THAT'S LIKE A HEROIN OD ANTIDOTE. I STILL DON'T KNOW WHO DID IT. THEY SAVED MY LIFE. BUT, I STILL ENDED UP IN A HOSPITAL. AND AFTER THAT...

OH MY GOD! MY BABY'S SHOOTING **HEROIN**!!

HOW DID YOU LET THINGS GET **SO BAD**?!

UM...YEAH. SO NOW I'M HERE.

OKAY. THANKS FOR SHARING, HANNAH. YOU SEE THAT YOU WERE OUT OF CONTROL. YOU YOURSELF SAID AS MUCH.

YEAH. SO?

SO...DO YOU THINK THAT YOU'LL **ALWAYS** BELIEVE THIS? I MEAN, WHEN YOU GET BACK TO THE "**REAL WORLD**"?

SURE. WHY NOT? I GET IT. WHY ALL THE DRAMA AND PAIN OF GOING TO MEETINGS AND SPONSORS AND STEPS?

I CAN ONLY SPEAK FOR M'SELF... I **NEED** THAT REMINDER, BECAUSE MY **WAY OF THINKING** HAS CHANGED SINCE I STARTED DRINKING AND DRUGGING LIKE I DID.

THAT'S WHAT THESE **MAINTENANCE STEPS** ARE ABOUT — THEY KEEP US **HONEST** TO OURSELVES AND **CHECK OUR THINKING**. IT'S FUNNY, NOW I'D ALMOST LIKE TO BELIEVE THAT I'D WANT THE PROGRAM EVEN **WITHOUT** BEING AN ADDICT! I'D EVEN HOLD ON TO **STEP ELEVEN**! IMAGINE THAT! ME, THE **ATHEIST**!

STEP ELEVEN
*"Sought through prayer and meditation to improve our conscious contact with God **as we understood Him**, praying only for knowledge of His will for us and the power to carry that out."*

123

125

YOU DON'T NEED ALL THAT CRAP HERE.

REMEMBER... THE *"MAGIC OF COMICS"*?!

K-SH.

ACTUALLY, IT'S GOOD THAT WE'RE HERE, ON THE MOON. IT GIVES US ANOTHER *PERSPECTIVE*.

ZZIP!

WHEN I WAS STILL ACTIVE IN MY ADDICTION, *A CORRECT PERSPECTIVE* OF MY SITUATION WAS WHAT I WAS LACKING. WE ALCOHOLICS AND ADDICTS SUFFER FROM THE INTERMINABLE MALADY OF *NOT SEEING THINGS* FOR WHAT THEY *ACTUALLY ARE*.

TAKE *HANNAH'S* SITUATION, FOR EXAMPLE. SHE'S LEARNED THE *STEPS* BY HEART. SHE'S SMART TOO. BUT SHE STILL NEEDS TO LEARN HOW TO *LIVE* AND WORK THE *STEPS* TO FIND A NEW *PERSPECTIVE*, A NEW WAY TO *SEE THE WORLD*!

THE FIRST PART OF RECOVERY IS *ADMISSION* OF *DEFEAT* AND SUBMISSION TO A POWER *GREATER* THAN *OURSELVES*. NEXT, IT'S ABOUT GAINING A *NEW PERSPECTIVE*...

126

...A PERSPECTIVE THAT, AFTER ALL, WE ARE NOT THE *CENTER OF THE UNIVERSE*.

127

IT'S NOT A REQUIREMENT TO HIT A **HOME RUN**, EITHER, LIKE SPENCER DID WITH THE MOON ROCK. RECOVERY IS FULL OF PEAKS AND VALLEYS — **LIKE LIFE!** IT'S LEARNING TO LIVE LIFE EACH DAY ON LIFE'S TERMS. THE STEPS GIVE US THE TOOLS AND THE GROUPS GIVE US THE SUPPORT TO GET THROUGH THE HARD TIMES — WHICH FREES US TO BE GRATEFUL FOR THE GOOD TIMES.

BUT THAT'S WHAT **REAL GRATITUDE** IS: IT'S NOT **HAVING WHAT YOU WANT.** IT'S **WANTING WHAT YOU GOT!** STILL, WE CAN USE OUR **IMAGINATION** AND **CREATIVITY** TO SEE IT ALL IN **A NEW LIGHT.**

PART OF THE JOY OF LIVING THE LIFE OF RECOVERY IS ACCEPTING LIFE ON ITS OWN TERMS — WITH ALL ITS REWARDS AND STRUGGLES. IT'S ABOUT EMBRACING SURPRISE. NOW AND THEN WE F—

WHAT? SP — **SPENCER...** **NOOOOOOO!**

SWIP!

WAAAH!!

WAAAH...!!!

EWIP!

SWUMP!

THUD!

Germany — October 1944

Wha— Where are we? Oh...we're here **again**... (*Spencer has a thing with WWII.*)

I see we're in Germany this time. Well, I suppose that's better than last time in the Pacific. What year is it, anyway? Oh…'44. The fall, I'd guess, looking at the state of things.

BOOM!

What was that?! Come boy, we'd better get out of here. Come on; I think I see some sort of compound over there.

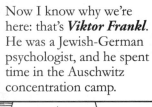

Of course, anyone who knows the truth knows that many died in the concentration camps. And, those who survived had seen horrific things. Human beings' capacity for cruelty, indeed, has no bounds...

CRACK

...yet our capacity for empathy, to *see the suffering of another and relate*, also is not limited.

In fact, a caring hand, reaching out to another, is often all we need to *keep going.* For Frankl, caring for others, helping them find *their own* purpose and meaning in life, became that which carried him through this time. He survived the war.

Dr. Frankl was so moved by the idea that *purpose and meaning* were a central part of what it means to be human that he developed an entire *psychological theory* around the idea — *logotherapy.*

Logotherapy is centered in the idea that meaning (from the Greek: *logos*) is the single most driving force in a person's life.

Recovery and Dr. Frankl's ideas are closely connected. The goal of Alcoholics Anonymous — to connect alcoholics with each other and give them a new purpose to life — is precisely what Frankl aimed to achieve.

It's *the solution* to our *problem.*

WELL...UM...I HAVE A QUESTION: I DON'T HAVE A PROBLEM DRINKING *NORMALLY*...SO WHAT IS *EXACTLY* THE *PROBLEM* YOU ALCOHOLICS HAVE?

AND WHAT'S THE *SOLUTION*?

WHOA. HE SPEAKS!

OKAY. THE *PROBLEM* IS EASY: WE HAVE A *DISEASE* OF THE BODY THAT CAUSES US TO LOSE CONTROL WHEN WE DRINK OR DRUG, AND AN *OBSESSION* OF THE *MIND* THAT CAUSES US TO DRINK AND DRUG. *WE CAN'T USE AND WE CAN'T QUIT.* THAT'S THE *POWERLESSNESS* THAT *STEP ONE* DESCRIBES: *"WE ADMITTED WE WERE POWERLESS OVER ALCOHOL [AND OTHER DRUGS] — THAT OUR LIVES HAD BECOME UNMANAGEABLE."* WE CAN'T DO ANYTHING ABOUT THE PHYSICAL ILLNESS; WE'LL HAVE THAT THE REST OF OUR LIVES. THAT MEANS THAT THE SOLUTION TO THIS PROBLEM HAS TO COME THROUGH OUR MINDS.

THE *SOLUTION* TO THAT *IRRECONCILABLE DILEMMA* IS THAT THE OTHER STEPS GIVE US A WAY TO RESTORE *PURPOSE AND MEANING* TO OUR LIVES; THE *MEANING* IS FOUND IN A POWER GREATER THAN OURSELVES THAT RELEASES US FROM OUR MENTAL OBSESSION WITH USING CHEMICALS. THE *PURPOSE* IS TO *PASS ON* THIS SOLUTION TO *OTHERS IN NEED*.

THE SIMPLICITY OF IT IS BRILLIANT. BEST OF ALL, SPENCER — *IT WORKS IF YOU WORK IT!!*

A **TWELVE STEP PROGRAM** IS INTENDED TO REPLACE ADDICTS' **DISTORTED** AND **DISEASED** THINKING. LET'S SEE WHAT OUR FRIENDS ARE TALKING ABOUT NOW...

...I HAD TO LEARN ALL OF THIS THE **HARD WAY**. UNFORTUNATELY, THIS IS THE CASE FOR MANY OF US: WE DON'T WANT SOBRIETY UNTIL **IT HURTS BADLY ENOUGH!**

OF COURSE, IT DOESN'T NEED TO BE THAT WAY. SOME PEOPLE ARE JUST **MORE HONEST WITH THEMSELVES** THAN OTHERS.

THAT'S WHAT THE BIG BOOK OF AA MEANS IN CHAPTER FIVE WHEN WE HEAR THAT RECOVERY IS AVAILABLE TO ANYONE WHO HAS **"THE CAPACITY TO BE HONEST."**

WHAT'S UP, MATT?

UH...I GOTTA COME CLEAN 'BOUT SOMETHING.

Y'KNOW ALL THAT SHIT I TOLD YA ABOUT ME GETTIN' AN AK-47 AND GETTIN' BUSTED BY THE COPS MAKIN' A STING? UH... THAT'S ALL BS. *TODO FUE MIERDA...*

WELL...LIKE I LEFT OFF...THINGS GOT BAD. I WAS A MESS.

YEAH...SO I SCORED A BUNCH OF CRYSTAL. IT WAS THE *SHI*— I MEAN...IT WAS *POWERFUL STUFF*. I WAS UP FOR *THREE DAYS* STRAIGHT. THE WHOLE TIME I WAS MAKING PLANS...

NOW THAT I THINK 'BOUT IT, I WAS TOTALLY *LOCO*!

I WAS THINKIN' THE WHOLE TIME THAT THE FEDS KNEW MY PLANS TO KILL ANTONIO. I DUNNO WHY. WELL, I GUESS THAT IT WAS NORMAL. SEEIN' AS HOW I WAS SHOOTIN' METH *CONSTANTLY*.

IT IS "NORMAL..." AT LEAST WHEN YOU'RE *THAT HIGH*!!

YOU GOT IT, BRO. I WAS STARTIN' TO GET THE BUGS ON MY ARMS. I STILL GOT SOME OF THE SCARS FROM PICKIN' AT 'EM.

YEAH...SO 'BOUT WHAT *REALLY* HAPPENED...

I WAS SO FUCKED UP. I THOUGHT I COULD DO ANYTHING. I WANTED TO KILL ANTONIO *THAT SAME NIGHT*.

135

BUT, Y'KNOW, I WASN'T EXACTLY IN THE BEST *FRAME OF MIND* TO REALLY DO ANYTHING.

I DIDN'T HAVE A GUN, A KNIFE, OR NOTHING. DUNNO WHAT I THOUGHT. WAS I SUPPOSED TO KILL ANTONIO WITH MY BARE HANDS?

HEY *CHOLOS*, WHERE'S ANTONIO?

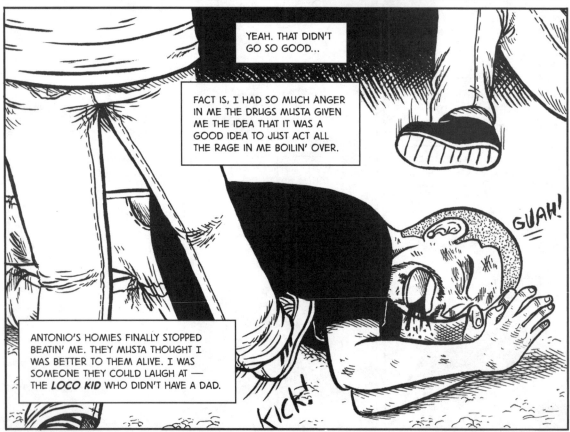

YEAH. THAT DIDN'T GO SO GOOD...

FACT IS, I HAD SO MUCH ANGER IN ME THE DRUGS MUSTA GIVEN ME THE IDEA THAT IT WAS A GOOD IDEA TO JUST ACT ALL THE RAGE IN ME BOILIN' OVER.

GUAH!

ANTONIO'S HOMIES FINALLY STOPPED BEATIN' ME. THEY MUSTA THOUGHT I WAS BETTER TO THEM ALIVE. I WAS SOMEONE THEY COULD LAUGH AT — THE *LOCO KID* WHO DIDN'T HAVE A DAD.

KICK!

WHAT HAPPENED THEN?

TO BE HONEST, NOTHIN' BIG — AT LEAST NOTHIN' LIKE I TOLD Y'ALL BEFORE.

I WAS STARTIN' TO COME DOWN OFF MY BINGE, BUT I COULDN'T SLEEP, EITHER. MY BRAIN WAS *CRASHIN'*. I HAD TO GET BACK UP. SO, I WENT TO MY DEALER. I DON'T KNOW WHAT I WOULDA DONE. I ONLY HAD MAYBE *TEN BUCKS* ON ME.

TURNS OUT, MY DEALER WASN'T AROUND...SO I DID THE ONLY THING I COULD THINK OF...

KNOCK! KNOC

I MUSTA LOOKED FOR HOURS. COULDN'T SEEM TO FIND NOTHIN'.

BUT I FINALLY FOUND SOMEONE.

YEAH. I SCORED SOME CHEAP CRYSTAL. NOT FOR LONG, ANYWAY.

I DID GET BUSTED BY THE COPS. THAT MUCH WAS TRUE.

BUT IT WAS A SIMPLE BUST. GUESS THEY WERE WATCHIN' THAT SPOT I WAS AT.

MY GRAMMA BAILED ME OUT. THEN SHE SENT ME HERE. I GUESS SHE HOPED I'D GET CLEANED UP. I DUNNO...I'M THINKING THAT...I DUNNO.

YOU CAN ALL CHEW ME UP AND SPIT ME OUT. I LIED.

HE-HE. SORRY. DON'T MEAN TO CHUCKLE. IT'S JUST THAT YOU REMIND ME OF *MYSELF*.

ME TOO, MATT. DO YOU THINK THAT YOU'RE *UNIQUE* IN THIS REGARD?

YEAH. WE'RE *ALL LIARS*, MATT. YOU'RE NOTHING SPECIAL. IT'S WHAT *ADDICTS DO*.

OUR LIVES ARE ALL ABOUT *DRAMA* AND THE LIES WE BUILT UP. WHAT'S FUNNY IS THAT I ACTUALLY BELIEVED THE LIES *I TOLD MYSELF*! THIS PROGRAM'S ABOUT HONESTY. I THINK IT MEANS THAT WE NEED TO LEARN THINGS WE DON'T *NORMALLY DO FOR OURSELVES*!

PERSONALLY, I THINK IT'S ABOUT GOD GIVING US *WHAT WE NEED* AT THE EXACT *TIME WE NEED IT*. IT'S ABOUT FINDING *THE KNOWLEDGE OF HIS WILL FOR US*.

BUT I DON'T BELIEVE NONE OF THAT SHIT! IT'S ALL JUS' *COINCIDENCE*!

MATT, LISTEN TO ME. I DON'T THINK YOU *REALLY* BELIEVE THAT. I THINK ACTUALLY WHAT YOU WANT IS *CONFIRMATION* THAT THERE ARE POWERS *BIGGER THAN YOU* AT WORK. GOD, COINCIDENCE, HIGHER POWER...WHATEVER YOU CALL IT: BE OPEN TO THE *POSSIBILITY* THAT YOU AREN'T THE *END ALL* OF YOUR EXISTENCE.

I GUESS — WHEN I'M HONEST 'BOUT IT — THAT BEFORE, WHEN I LEFT YOU GUYS TO BE BY MYSELF, I WAS WONDERING HOW I WAS GONNA BAIL THIS PLACE.

BUT, Y'KNOW...ALL O' THE SUDDEN, *DEBBY* SHOWS UP. THE *ONE PERSON* I DON'T WANNA TALK TO...NOT ONLY THAT, *SHE WANTS TO MAKE THINGS RIGHT*!!

THAT'S THE THING I STARTED NOTICING. YOU GUYS ARE *JUS' LIKE ME*. I'M NOT STUPID. I CAN SEE THAT THIS *TWELVE STEPS* THING IS ABOUT GETTING PEOPLE TO LET GO OF BEIN' IN CHARGE, TO FINALLY ADMIT WE'RE POWERLESS. Y'GOTTA UNDERSTAND, THOUGH: I DON'T DO THAT VERY EASY. IT AIN'T *EASY* GIVIN' UP. IT ALSO AIN'T EASY TO SEE THAT I'M NOT THE *CENTER* OF WHAT I WANNA DO IN MY LIFE.

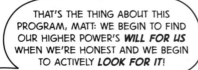

THAT'S THE THING ABOUT THIS PROGRAM, MATT: WE BEGIN TO FIND OUR HIGHER POWER'S **WILL FOR US** WHEN WE'RE HONEST AND WE BEGIN TO ACTIVELY **LOOK FOR IT**!

BY THE WAY...YOU SHOULD BE PROUD OF YOURSELF. NOT MANY COME TO HONESTY WITH THEMSELVES AS QUICKLY AS YOU. IT'S THE NATURE OF OUR **DISEASE**, I SUPPOSE. **IT** JUST WANTS US TO **STAY SICK**.

I'VE HEARD THIS BEFORE, ABOUT ADDICTION BEING A **DISEASE**. IN MY OPINION, IT'S COUNTERPRODUCTIVE TO REFER TO IT AS THAT.

DISEASES ARE HEART DISEASE OR CANCER OR THE STOMACH FLU. THEY ARE THINGS THAT JUST HAPPEN TO PEOPLE. IT'S NOT THEIR **FAULT**.

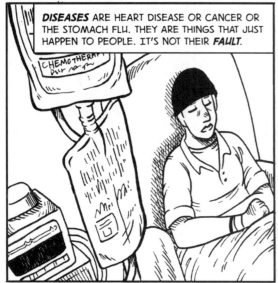

MY ADDICTION...AND ALL THAT I DID — THAT'S **MY FAULT**. THAT'S NOT A **DISEASE**!!

GOOD POINT, HANNAH. BUT LET ME ASK YOU SOMETHING...

DID YOU EVER **INTEND** ON **RUINING YOUR LIFE** AND ENDING UP IN TREATMENT FOR DRUG AND ALCOHOL ADDICTION?

WELL...NO. BUT THAT DOESN'T MEAN IT **WASN'T** MY FAULT!

I'M NOT SPEAKING TO YOUR **CULP-ABILITY**...OR THE **CONSEQUENCES** OF YOUR ACTIONS. I'M ASKING WHETHER OR NOT YOU **PLANNED** ON **ENDING UP HERE** WHEN YOU STARTED TO **DRINK** AND **DRUG**.

WELL...I SUPPOSE NOT. BUT—

141

YOU GOTTA UNDERSTAND WHAT THEY WERE FIGHTING **BACK THEN**: PEOPLE EVERYWHERE WERE **ASHAMED** NOT ONLY OF WHAT THEY DID, BUT ALSO OF **WHO THEY WERE**. BEING AN ALCOHOLIC WAS LIKE A **RED MARK** IN THEIR LIVES!

AND LET ME TELL YOU... PROBABLY MORE THAN ANYTHING ELSE, **SHAME** IS WHAT MAKES ADDICTION SO **DEADLY**.

YOU GOT THAT RIGHT. SHAME KILLS.

WHAT IS WHAT WE HAVE THEN? IS IT A DISEASE, A MENTAL ILLNESS TURNED ON BY DRUGS AND ALCOHOL, OR IS IT **SOMETHIN' ELSE**?

IT'S LIKE A HOUSE, STANDING AROUND OTHER HOMES. IT DOESN'T MATTER WHAT COLOR YOU SAY IT IS; IF THE INTERIOR IS FILLED WITH ROTTING WOOD AND BAD WIRING IT'S STILL GONNA BE **CONDEMNED AND NEED REPAIR**.

WHATEVER YOU CALL ADDICTION, WHAT'S THE CURE?

THERE IS NO CURE AS OF YET — IT'S A CHRONIC ILLNESS THAT NEEDS TO BE MANAGED, LIKE DIABETES. BUT THERE'S A **SPIRITUAL SOLUTION** IN THE **TWELVE STEPS**. THE **FINAL STEP** SUMS UP WHAT IT'S ALL ABOUT:

STEP TWELVE
*"Having had
a spiritual awakening
as the result of these steps,
we tried to carry
this message to alcoholics,
and to practice these principles
in all our affairs."*

CAREFUL SPENCE... THAT FALL WOULD BE A DOOZY.

!!

STAYING SOBER IS KIND OF LIKE A TIGHTROPE ACT. ANY OF US CAN FALL AT ANY TIME. IT REQUIRES VIGILANCE.

BUT, WE SHOULDN'T LET THIS GET US DOWN ABOUT RECOVERY. THE **SOLUTION** TO OUR ILLNESS ISN'T SOMETHING MEANT TO **DRAG US DOWN**. IN THE SAME VEIN, **TWELVE STEP RECOVERY** IS REALLY ABOUT **WAKING UP** TO WHAT OUR CONDITION IS...

...**A SPIRITUAL PROBLEM.** REMEMBER, **SPIRITUAL THINGS** AREN'T THE SAME AS **RELIGION**. RELIGION CAN HAVE **SPIRITUALITY** CONNECTED WITH IT, AND MANY PEOPLE DO FIND THEIR SPIRITUALITY IN A CHURCH. WHAT I'M SAYING IS THAT OUR DIFFICULTY AS ADDICTS IS CONNECTED DIRECTLY WITH OUR **DIS-EASE**. WE ALCOHOLICS AND ADDICTS ARE NOT "**AT-EASE**" — NOT AT ALL!

TO FEEL "**AT-EASE**" WE NEED EITHER: (1) DRUGS AND ALCOHOL, WHICH EVENTUALLY **KILL** US, OR (2) A SPIRITUAL PATH TO **SEREN-ITY** AND **WELLNESS**. SO THE TWELVE STEPS ARE REALLY ABOUT **LIFE**! BILL W. SAID IT BEST WHEN HE SUMMED UP THE TWELVE STEPS IN THE DESCRIPTION TO THE LAST STEP. HE WROTE: "**THE JOY OF LIVING IS THE THEME OF A.A.'S TWELFTH STEP, AND ACTION IS ITS KEY WORD... [IN ACTIVELY WORKING THE STEPS,] WE HAVE EACH FOUND SOMETHING CALLED A SPIRITUAL AWAKENING.**"

IT'S NOT JUST AA THAT LOOKS AT IT THIS WAY. **NA, GA, AL-ANON,** AND **ANY** OTHER **TWELVE STEP GROUP** SEES IT LIKE THIS TOO.

GASP!

AAH!!

AH... WHA— OH...

OH. IGNORE HIM. HE'LL BE FINE. Y'KNOW HOW IT IS — *ARTISTS AND THEIR DRAMA.*

OH...BY THE WAY...THERE'S A *GREAT WAY* TO *REMEMBER* THE *TWELVE STEPS.* IT WAS SOMETHING I LEARNED WHEN I FIRST *GOT SOBER.*

IT HELPS TO SEE THAT ALL THE STEPS ARE *PAIRED OFF TOGETHER.*

IT'S LIKE THIS...

...2 & 3, 4 & 5, 6 & 7, 8 & 9, 10 & 11...

...AND *STEP ONE* IS CONNECTED WITH *STEP TWELVE.*

EACH STEP IS CONNECTED WITH THE OTHER AS A PAIR. EACH IS PAIRED AS A SET OF *BELIEF AND ACTION.* FOR EXAMPLE, *STEP TWO* IS ABOUT COMING TO A BELIEF AND TAKING ACCOUNT THAT THERE MIGHT BE A HIGHER POWER TO RESTORE US TO SANITY. AND *STEP THREE* IS ABOUT TAKING ACTION FROM TWO: WE MAKE A DECISION TO TURN OUR WILL AND OUR LIVES OVER TO GOD *AS WE UNDERSTAND HIM.*

AND *ONE AND TWELVE?* YUP. THAT'S THE *FIRST (AND LAST) PAIR!* IF YOU REMEMBER THE STEPS THIS WAY, I THINK YOU'LL FIND THEY AREN'T AS SCARY — AFTER ALL, IT'S JUST *SIX* THINGS TO REMEMBER INSTEAD OF *TWELVE!*

145

*God, grant me
the SERENITY
to accept the things
I cannot change,
COURAGE
to change the things
I can, and
WISDOM
to know the difference.*

WELL...WHAT DO WE DO NOW?

DUNNO ABOUT YOU, HANNAH-GIRL, BUT I'M HEADIN' BACK TO MY SOBER HOUSE AFTER THIS. GOTTA GET UP FOR A MEETING. I'LL BE HEADIN' BACK TO MY JOB IN LONDON NEXT WEEK.

MANY OF YOU ARE JUST BEGINNING TO GET WHAT THE **TWELVE STEPS** ARE AND HOW THEY SEND US INTO ACTION. REMEMBER THAT THE ULTIMATE GOAL IS THAT YOU HAVE YOUR **OWN LIVES TO LEAD**. YOU NEED TO WORK THEM TO **KEEP YOURSELVES HEALTHY**.

OF COURSE, I HOPE ALL OF YOU HAVE A SPONSOR. YOU KNOW THAT'S A **VITAL** PART OF YOUR RECOVERY. WE GOTTA WORK WITH ANOTHER.

GOOD POINT, DEBBY! I ALMOST FORGOT TO MENTION THAT; I'M GLAD YOU DID. WHAT'S REALLY GREAT IS SOME OF THESE PEOPLE BECOME **MORE THAN SIMPLY FRIENDS**. SPONSORS CAN BECOME A CONFIDANT WITH WHOM YOU CAN REALLY GROW IN CONTINUING TO WORK THE STEPS. I KEEP IN TOUCH WITH CONNOR, MY SPONSOR, TO THIS DAY!

HEY, GUYS...THANKS FOR SHARING YOUR LIVES WITH ME. KEEP IT SIMPLE. STAY THE COURSE. I'LL LOOK FORWARD TO SEEING YOU ALL AGAIN SOMEDAY...**SOBER.**

147

Afterword

If I were able to travel back in time to 2009 to encounter the Dan Maurer who was then mired in his addiction, I probably would not have been able to change the path I inevitably took. It's likely that I still would have made the same choices. Why? Because when addiction is active, it trumps any other possible decision-making process an addict might have.

In truth, even if I could have laid out the facts directly to my past self ...

> You're going to ruin your life this year with your alcohol and other drug use. Then you're going to go through agonizing withdrawal from benzodiazepines for eight long months. In the meantime, you'll need to learn how to live again. But don't worry, you're going to get a new spirituality, and you'll strive to serve others like you never have before.

... it wouldn't have mattered. I still would have thought that I could control my destiny, because being "in control" was what I was about; however, the opposite was true—I was out of control.

Looking back, I have wondered what my life and career path would have been like had I not made the choices I did. I regret the path I took, especially the pain I caused others. However, I am only where I am today *because I made my mistakes and I had the support to learn the Twelve Steps of recovery.* That's something that nonaddicts can never understand, why so many recovering alcoholics and addicts are grateful for being what they are, for having the illness they have. What others see as a weakness and flaw, we see as the source of power within our fellowship in AA, NA, or any other Twelve Step group.

If readers who are on the journey of recovery gain nothing else from the experience of entering into the world of *Sobriety: A Graphic Novel,* let it be this: Your story is not yet finished; through the power of the Twelve Steps you too can find your true self and, in the process, discover that you have the opportunity to be a gift to others who are as of yet still suffering the pain of addiction. It is my hope that the medium of comic art can convey this hopeful message to all who want to find their purpose and meaning.

About the Author

Daniel D. Maurer was an ELCA-ordained minister for eleven years, serving churches in western North Dakota, and is now a freelance writer. In addition to *Sobriety: A Graphic Novel,* Daniel is author of the book *Faraway: One Suburban Kid's Story as a Victim of Sex Trafficking* and is published with the Alban Institute, the United Methodist publication *The Upper Room,* and Sparkhouse, the ecumenical outreach of Augsburg Fortress Publishers. He is also a contributing writer for the Loft Literary Center in Minneapolis.

Daniel lives openly in recovery and frequently speaks to the power of the Twelve Steps in his life. He lives with his family in St. Paul, Minnesota.

For more info, please visit www.danthestoryman.com.

About the Illustrator

Spencer Amundson, a graduate of the Minneapolis College of Art and Design, is a freelance comic artist and illustrator. He is from Sioux Falls, South Dakota, and lives in Minneapolis.